THE
LUSTY
VEGAN

THE LUSTY VEGAN

A COOKBOOK AND RELATIONSHIP MANIFESTO FOR VEGANS AND THE PEOPLE WHO LOVE THEM

AYINDÉ HOWELL AND ZOË EISENBERG

VEGAN HERITAGE PRESS
Woodstock • Virginia

ISBN 13: 978-0-9854662-9-9

First Edition, October 2014

10 9 8 7 6 5 4 3 2 1

Vegan Heritage Press, LLC books are available at quantity discounts. For information, please visit our website at www.veganheritagepress.com or write the publisher at Vegan Heritage Press, P.O. Box 628, Woodstock, VA 22664-0628.

Library of Congress Cataloging-in-Publication Data

Howell, Ayinde

The lusty vegan : a cookbook and relationship manifesto for vegans and the people who love them / Ayinde Howell and Zoe Eisenberg. -- First edition.

pages cm

Includes index.

ISBN 978-0-9854662-9-9 (print) -- ISBN 978-0-9889492-5-6 (epub ebook) -- ISBN 978-0-9889492-6-3 (prc ebook) 1. Vegan cooking. 2. Veganism. 3. Interpersonal relations. I. Eisenberg, Zoe II. Title.

TX837.H6969 2014

641.5'636--dc23

2014022438

Cover and interior photography by Geoff Souder

Food styling by Ayindé Howell

Cover design by Dianne Wenz

Disclaimer: The information provided in this book should not be taken as medical advice. If you require a medical diagnosis or prescription, or if you are contemplating any major dietary change, please consult a qualified health-care provider. You should always seek an expert medical opinion before making changes in your diet or supplementation regimen.

Vegan Heritage Press books are published by Vegan Heritage Press, LLC and distributed by Andrews McMeel Publishing.

Printed in the United States of America

Dedication

ZOË: For my parents, who always encouraged me to be myself, and taught me from an early age to appreciate the lentil.

AYINDÉ: This is for my family, who rarely understand my methods, but love and support me no matter what. Especially for my parents, who had a vision to change the world with a piece of tofu. I'm doing my part.

Contents

WTF IS A LUSTY VEGAN?

"WTF is a lusty vegan?"

Right now you may be thinking, okay, what the f*ck is a Lusty Vegan? A hemp-clad protester who desperately needs to get laid? A glossy-lipped semi-lebrity covered in lettuce? A kale fanatic littering your social media feeds with food porn?

Sure, some of us may fall into those stereotypes, but let's take it further. Lusty Vegans are vegans who are looking for love. We are just as passionate about what is on our plates as we are about what is in our hearts and who is sliding in between our sheets. Lusty Vegans put the passion in compassion, and we're finding that our unique lifestyles often affect our love lives. Why? Because food, like love and sex, is important. It's nourishing, it's uplifting, it's emotional, and—like the relationship status of doom—it's complicated.

Why you need to read this book

If you're rolling your eyes and thinking "how can dating a vegan be that complex? It's just food," well then chew on this: Mealtime is important. Eating satisfies our most primal need, but remember that we also have emotional ties to what we eat. We still love what our mothers cooked for us, we know just what to eat to cure a broken heart, and we all have our individual guilty pleasures.

FOOD, LIKE LOVE AND SEX, IS IMPORTANT.
IT'S NOURISHING, IT'S UPLIFTING, IT'S EMOTIONAL,

AND--LIKE THE RELATIONSHIP STATUS OF DOOM--

IT'S COMPLICATED.

We have a strong bond with what we eat, yet these ties are easy to overlook—until you are forced to think about them every time you sit at a table.

When you sit down for a meal, you're making a choice that has a large reflection on who you are as a person. From emotional ties to nutritional and philosophical beliefs, your food choices say a lot about you. When dating someone whose relationship with food and philosophical beliefs directly oppose yours, you are called to pause and think about just how different you are. Whether it's eating in your cramped apartment on TV trays set for two, or eating out in a group with friends, the meal is definitive. Navigating those definitive mo-

ments with someone whose opposing beliefs are displayed three times a day at mealtime can be tricky.

Veganism on and off the plate

In case you don't already know, veganism is a lifestyle based on a belief that all sentient beings are equal. While people go vegan for a variety of reasons (we'll get into those later), the incentive is usually tethered to the founding principal of non-harming and equality. It's not a diet. It's an alternative way of thinking and acting. This means that the differences between a vegan and an omnivore extend far beyond the dinner plate. However, this is a cookbook, guys! So for the most part, we will be focusing on the yummier side of things—the mealtime dilemmas and basic lifestyle disparities that occur during what we have come to call "divided" relationships. We're going to let you field the philosophical differences on your own. That being said, it's important to acknowledge that the differences we discuss here are rooted in a philosophy that goes much deeper than an aversion to dairy. Whew.

Who are we?

This book is authored by two vegans. We tag team the narrative, and we trust you'll be able to keep up. One of us—a veteran restaurant-trained vegan chef and founder of iEatGrass.com—has been vegan all his life. The other, a spunky, potty-mouthed writer, has been a vegan for her entire adult life, and was a cheese-addicted vegetarian for most of her adolescence (is Cheddar Anonymous a thing?).

Here's the catch: neither one of us has ever dated another vegan.

Crazy, right?! However, we've discovered we're not alone. Most of the vegans we know have never had the opportunity to keep it veg in the bedroom either. Finding two vegans in a relationship is like spotting a leprechaun on a unicorn giving out free tickets to a Michael Jackson concert. So if we're not dating each other, who are we dating? Everybody else. This is where it gets... complicated.

In this book, we break down our possible couple pairings into three major camps:

1. **Vegan on omnivore:** For the dreamy-eyed vegan dating a meat-eater. The vegan is most likely hatching a plan for converting their omni.

2. **Omnivore on vegan:** "Everything eaters" who have found themselves in a relationship with a vegan, yet remain a bit clueless or skeptical about the lifestyle.

3. **Vegan on vegan:** The nearly mythical occurrence of two vegans dating one another. Cross your fingers for vegan baby making!

Where did this book come from?

As a young executive chef and bachelor living in Manhattan, Ayindé spent years cooking a ton of delicious plant-based food for his clientele, his friends, and his lady friends. At some point, like clockwork, his vegan lifestyle would become an issue in his romantic relationships. Over the years, his dates shared similar laments and queries, including "Wait, you don't even eat butter?" and "I'd cook for you, but you can't eat anything!"

Ayindé may have had ninety-nine problems, but cooking amazing vegan food was definitely not one. Determined that his girlfriends would at least eat vegan while in his house, Ayindé's recipe repertoire began to grow exponentially.

In 2010, Chef Ayindé was tapped to write a weekly column for a popular food blog in New York. He began to talk about his then-current relationship challenges with a woman we will meet later in this book. His juicy tidbits about his love life and innovative recipes would literally get him stopped at parties by folks wanting to know what happened next with them and what the next recipe was. However, his editors wanted less love life and more tofu talk, so he put the idea on the proverbial back burner.

That's where this project had been simmering until he met Zoë, who had also been writing about the convergence of love, sex, and food on her own personal blog. Talk about a meeting of the minds! With our separate romantic experiences in mind, we had both been unofficially researching the whole inter-palate dating dilemma for a long time before we decided to co-write a book about it. More on that later.

Ayindé hired Zoë as the first-ever iEatGrass.com intern, and as iEat-Grass grew, she made her way through the ranks to Managing Editor. Ayindé punted the whole vegan dating idea to Zoë, and we turned it into a weekly column on iEatGrass called, you guessed it, The Lusty Vegan. There, Zoë tackled all things sex, love, and food politics. While Zoë wrote, Ayindé continued his "field research" as a chef and boyfriend/lover/homieloverfriend—creating countless meals with his omnivorous lady friends in mind.

After years of incredible eating, tons of funny stories, and great input from our readers, we are excited to bring you our findings. We are bursting with recipes, tips, and anecdotes for vegans and omnivores alike—for the everyday folks new to this vegan par-tay and for the person who thinks quinoa is bird food, but loves that quinoa-fed vegan booty. Since we have studied omnis so closely—biblically, even—trust us that the advice is sound.

We will cover all sorts of ripe material, like how cohabiting vegans and omnivores can traverse a divided kitchen, and how omnis can keep your new vegan fox happy without donning a hemp sweater and harvesting wheat grass in your bathtub.

We share our own personal and often embarrassing learning experiences, like the time Ayindé threatened to break up with his girlfriend if she ate chicken; she went ahead and ate it anyway. In bed. Out of a box that had "fried chicken" written on it. In the Food for Sex chapter, Zoë guiltily admits to fetishizing the way her boyfriend ate ice cream made of...wait for it...cow's milk! (Gasp.) We implore you to learn from our mistakes and use our experiences to help you navigate the pitfalls and pioneer your own romantic success in this brave new world. Let's start at the beginning and introduce ourselves.

AYINDÉ: Hi, I'm a lifelong vegan. Yes, all my life. No, I have never eaten meat. My parents were vegan, and they raised me to be the same. I have also been an executive chef and restaurant owner for the past fifteen years. Most of my friends and every woman I've dated have been "regular people" or "omnivores," as we have come to call them. Growing up as The Vegan Kid On The Block was always weird. In fact that's where the name iEatGrass comes from—kids who used to ask if that's what vegans eat. It seems today, just thirty some years later, the national conversation is leaning toward health and healthy plant-based food. So who's the weird one now? Still me? Okay...cool.

As an adult I have become the homie who can cook. All of my friends and girlfriends loved to come by my restaurant or invite themselves over for dinner. I love to cook, so it's nothing to whip them up something tasty, whether they're vegan or not. My friends always say, "I'd be vegan if I could eat like this every day." In my early dating years, I never really saw a problem with dating omnivores—different lifestyles were not as important as a big booty. As I grew older, I started to think differently about what I wanted. I began looking for more meaningful relationships—as in, my fingers are crossed for a life partner. Hopefully, she will be vegan...with a big booty. What? I like what I like, I'm not judging *you*.

Around the time my relationship goals shifted, I started teaching more, and specifically teaching people how to make vegan food in a different way; simple always works best. Most of this thinking occurred during my last real relationship. We had a lot of meals together, and I learned a lot about myself as a person, a chef, and a great boyfriend. Seriously, what?

During that last infamous relationship, I came up with some pretty great and approachable recipes, one of which—my enchiladas—was published in *The New York Times*. I actually shot the photo for it in my ex's apartment. I've included a couple other dishes in this book that were featured in various publications. Most of the recipe ideas came from our weekly Sunday dinner dates during which I, the vegan, was catering to my girlfriend's omnivorous palate. Oftentimes she would suggest one of her favorite meals for me to translate into something we could both eat. Since I was a chef, she became the "regular" in my apartment bistro. I would attempt to get the familiar flavor and texture profiles and keep her worldly palate excited. The result was a diverse collection of recipes.

ZOË: Hi there. While I'm not a lifelong vegan like Ayindé, I've been eschewing meat since puberty, and finally ditched dairy in college. I haven't looked back. I'm a writer, lover, and veggie fiend, and I like to talk endlessly about my two favorite things—food and sex.

I have been embracing positive sexuality for even longer than I've been embracing the bulk food section of the health food store. Life is simply too short to waste your time with bad sex and undercooked noodles.

I'm also a bit of a serial monogamist, and I'm into commitment on the culinary level too. I've been happily eating oatmeal every morning for the past decade, and the idea of socializing with one man-part for the rest of my life—while terrifying or boring for others—is exciting to me. If I dig the fit and feel, why look elsewhere?

Dick aesthetics aside, food has always been heavily present in my relationships. I once dated a guy who only ate bacon and tuna salad. In this book, I adoringly refer to him as "Tuna," and I swear his eating habits were a huge reason behind our break up. That, and an incident involving jealousy (his), pyromania (his), and a 1995 Honda Civic (mine).

The reason Ayindé and I bonded in the first place, and the reason I snagged my internship with iEatGrass back in 2010, is because we naturally connected over the idea that vegans care about more than animal rights and pressing tofu. While those things are important (I like my tofu extra chewy, since you asked), I can't stress enough that vegans, like everybody else, have other interests and hobbies. I care about art, film, politics, food, love, and sex. I don't care for sports or country music, but everything else is pretty much fair game. While we vegans may be more highly evolved (ahem) than the average American McDonald's patron, overall, all I want is a little love and understanding—just like everybody else. Ayindé and I get it, and we hope you do too.

Why don't we just shut up and date each other?

Har, har, har. [blank stare] We're addressing this here because we know eventually you're going to ask. And we don't totally blame you; when two single vegans co-write a book in which they talk about not being able to find other single vegans, well, it's clearly a question begging to be asked. The answer is simple: We don't have that kind of connection. We have an awesome creative, collaborative, let's-write-a-cookbook, high-five and eat some Bibimbap connection. Also, we work together. Now excuse us while we ask why you don't go date your co-workers. Sheesh.

If you're vegan...

Then you already know that finding a mate with a compatible lifestyle can be difficult. As of 2012, it was estimated that around 2 percent of Americans are vegans.

That means unless you want to stand outside your farmer's market with a sign that says "meat-free sausage?" it may be hard to run into another vegan. And even if you do, who's to say you are attracted to them? And if you are, then who's to say they are single? The good ones go faster than free tequila at a dive bar. And more importantly, who's to say they are not hemp-clad, patchouli-smelling, card-carrying Burning Man types? Not that there's anything wrong with that. I'm always

saying that weird is good. But let's face it: Most people don't want to hang around someone they think is "abnormal." An original, sure. "Abnormal," maybe not. Ayindé can tell you. He was raised vegan, and if you think being vegan in small town America in the eighties was cool, you are sorely mistaken. It's bad enough being a hormonal teen with braces and gangly limbs. Imagine explaining veganism to the lunchroom bully or your high school crush...

"You see, mayonnaise is made from eggs, which come from a chicken, and I don't agree with...wait...where are you going?"

To help you and your partner see eye-to-eye (and plate-to-plate), we have paired an aperitif of advice on how to coexist in your vegan-fusion relationship with delish recipes that will keep your partner from dreaming about bacon while they gag down mouthfuls of your steamed Swiss chard. Time to step it up! No more steaming your greens. How can you impress anybody with that? Ayindé is releasing some of his most coveted recipes in this book, a bounty of drool-worthy plant-based fare that will have your partner suspiciously searching the kitchen for hidden take-out boxes. Truth.

If you're omnivore...

And you're alive in the twenty-first century, then you have probably heard about this vegan stuff. Maybe you think it's a trend. (Trust us, it's not.) Maybe you're turned off by some of the crazier activism antics. Like all extremist groups, the extreme side of the vegan world can give the rest of us a bad rap, so we promise you, we're not all into angry banners and naked protests...well, naked yes, protest no.

If you've fallen for a vegan, you are entering a crazy new world of nutritional yeast and alkaline diets. Don't worry. We're here to help you make heads, tails, and breakfast for your new bae. What's better, we're going to do it without offending your new girl when you plan a surprise trip to the zoo or buy your guy a bag of marshmallows to make s'mores on your romantic camping trip. Wait, what? Vegans don't like zoos or s'mores?! Don't worry, we're here to help you understand these small nuances. Think of us as your vegan wing-men. While vegans are still a slim population, there are millions of us, and most are between the ages of eighteen and thirty-five—the prime age for prowling.

With veganism growing, and more veg-curious folks popping up every day, it's really no surprise that you are dating one of us. Who can blame you? Most of us can cook, and we take care our bodies, which means we're foxy as f*ck and beasts in bed. Some even say we taste better. (Psst! We do.) But if the thought of a life without cheese makes you want to cry, and you never think twice about buying a nice pair of leather shoes, then you're gonna run into trouble in your vegan romance. Yes, heads up, your shoes will become an issue in a conversation one day. Save the shoes! You've been warned.

The truth about vegans in stereo(type)

There are somewhere around 2 million vegans in the world, and that number is growing. As with any subculture, there are sub-subcultures. To get you up to speed, we're going to use a popular, albeit unorthodox, method of stereotyping - because if you can't laugh at yourself, someone else surely will.

Here is a rundown of the top six types of vegans you might meet in the wild:

- ethical vegans (see: Ingrid Newkirk)
- environmental vegans (follow the scent of patchouli)
- veganish (this is Oprah's doing)
- pop vegans (read: millennials)
- sentenced-to-veganism vegans (two words: Bill Clinton)
- health-obsessed vegans (possibly also raw, gluten-free, grain-free, soy-free, salt-free, fun-free. Womp womp)

Got it? Good! Okay, enough with the stereotyping! Let's get to the juicy stuff, beginning with a common emotion we all feel or have felt. Hint: It's a four-letter word. No, not love, but …

Lust [lʌst]: An emotion or feeling of intense desire. You can lust for knowledge, power, food, or the body of another. Lust is an important part of a relationship; it keeps us coming back for seconds. And thirds. And for us commitment types, for 70,000ths. But most people, vegans or not, desire a connection that extends beyond the fun we have in bed. How far will lust get you when you're old and wrinkly? Let's all imagine that…. yeah, not sure why we went there. Oh yes, because when those of us who stay together for good (less than 50 percent nowadays) are old and bat-shit crazy, the only thing left is…

Love [lʌv]: We all need love, and fostering a deep bond is important. Bonding is encouraged by serotonin, a chemical we produce that is an important part of our body's make-up. They call it a chemical attraction for a reason—some scientists believe we actually pick our partners by smell. Thanks a lot, pheromones. Maybe I don't WANT to go for the unstable, flakey, creative type who can write a whole screenplay in a week but can't remember to call me, yet again.

Unfortunately, we can't choose whom we fall in love with. Science or not, those ooey-gooey feelings usually hit us like the winter up North. One moment you're doing your thing, and the next, there's a storm comin' and you've got it bad. You're canceling plans with friends to stay in and stare at each other. You're leaving your holy sanctuary others refer to as "the couch," and following your new girl to her 5:00 AM spin class. You're listening to your guy's heavy metal when you typically prefer Bach. Two months in, you look down to realize you're both wearing matching skinny jean/vest combos. Yikes!

But at some point, those love-induced opiates will wear off, and you will see that while your girl may have the perfect ass, nobody is actually perfect. And when you come across bumps caused by your differences, then you figure it out. And by "figure it out," we mean the C word...

No no, the other C word:

Compromise [ˈkɒmprəˌmaɪz]: The dreaded C word, often used as a weapon in arguments, is defined as a settlement of differences in which each side makes concessions.

Compromising on where the TV goes or finally agreeing to get rid of your collection of boob "art" is one thing. You might even change religions for the right person. But when it comes to food, it's a whole other ball game. Jesus to Buddha, Republican to Democrat, Red Sox to Yankees—not an issue. But bacon to tofu?! We are gonna need some help here.

Fact is, we don't scientifically understand human attraction. Space travel and nuclear bombs, no biggie. But whether it's a bad boy in a (p)leather jacket or a big booty in great jeans, we still don't know what makes us drawn to another person. There are theories, and we can psychoanalyze and sniff each other's stinky t-shirts until we're Freuded out, but we probably still won't understand why we like who we like.

Eff it! Add it to the list of things we just don't understand, like the middle seat on airplanes, or why old people announce when they have to go to the bathroom. Whomever you love, you love. If you're vegan, if you're omni—you can't help your attraction to one another. And you shouldn't have to. Because when it comes to your relationship, food, and your sex life, it's best to keep it simple. It should taste great and be satisfying. Nobody asks for seconds of plain steamed broccoli, or to get it in the missionary position for the third...time...this...week. Yawn.

What will you find in this book?

With *The Lusty Vegan*, we're creating a unique experience; everybody wants to be a special snowflake, right? We're no different, except that we want to be a helpful special snowflake. We want you to walk away with a greater understanding of how you can coexist with a person who has different ideals and values than you, with a wealth of recipes (from simple and satisfying to super-fancy kitchen-ninja impress-everybody status) and a sense of accomplishment because you finished this awesome book and f*ck yeah for personal growth!

You will be reading stories from both of us, learning how to navigate your vegan/omnivore relationship with minimal food politics spats and flying cutlery and maximum hearty, wholesome, "I can't believe this is vegan" meals that every palate will enjoy. We hope that you will learn from our past experiences—or at least be entertained and amused.

REMEMBER: YOU CAN'T BULLY SOMEONE INTO THINKING YOUR WAY IS THE RIGHT WAY, AND WHY WOULD YOU WANT TO?

Stories from the field

Peppered throughout the book are stories and tips from some of our friends, like sweet vegan baker and cookbook author Hannah Kaminsky, Discerning Brute and Brave Gentleman founder Joshua Katcher, Girlie Girl Army's own Chloé Jo Davis, and more. Each of the vegan all-stars featured in the book explores a different outlook on love and life, and a different wealth of experience, and we're happy to be able to share them with you. You're welcome.

Since this book is meant to be a powerhouse of condensed info, we wanted to give you as many useful morsels as possible, and so in terms of relationship and dating resources, we also opened it up to our iEatGrass.com readers and our social media networks, allowing fellow vegans and omnivores to give us their most tried-and-true tips for dating one another. Because these tips, suggestions, and ideas come from so many different noggins, some of them naturally oppose one another. This only makes it more fun.

Learning to cook, Ayindé's way

Ayindé here. With fifteen plus years under my belt as a restaurant chef, I have learned a couple of things. First, the French have one thing down: fat carries flavor. In traditional French cooking, they use tons of butter from a cow's milk or animal fat. The second thing I have learned from the French is that they are not afraid to go for it, and eat with reckless abandon. In this book, I borrow from the French and use plant-based fats to achieve the same goal: superior flavor. Some of the heartier, more complex recipes in this book use a healthy amount of oil or vegan butter. In getting feedback from my rockstar recipe testers, I learned that the use of oil is shocking to some. Veganism is, and should be, a healthy choice by default. I am using plant-based fats in these recipes and no trans fats or animal fats. Fat is a part of every balanced diet, and an essential part of cooking. Healthy fats are also essential for your organs to properly function, from your brain to your sex parts. So, instead of changing all my recipes to blend in with all the rest, because I'm a badass (which is what got me this cookbook deal in the first place), I ask you this: if you see a recipe with more oil than you typically use, try it the way I make it first. It's all in the technique.

When you boil it down, cooking is simple: if you have fire, some good plants, and something sharp, you can eat. I try to stray from this as little as possible. Fancy food is great, and I cover some of that, but I want to give you recipes that you can actually make and feel proud of. I want you to serve up recipes you can make without having to blow your paycheck on ingredients you can't pronounce and will probably only use once.

I cut my teeth working in restaurant kitchens and at home learning at the stove with my parents. Many of the most important moments in my life have happened in a kitchen, and I tell some of those stories with each recipe. As you learn these recipes and build your own stories, know that failing is a part of mastery. The happy mistake is often the key to whole other worlds. I have learned techniques that are as important as any ingredients, and I will be sharing what I have learned with you. I suggest this book be used as part of your vegan cookbook collection. Revisit it often for unique and satisfying main dishes and robust flavors. Keep on reading the books of my colleagues to round out the plate; veganism has come a long way since the days of one good book. But keep ours on top of the stack.

Cooking terms

Below is a list of terms that I use in many of my recipes. Listing them once makes it easier than repeating eighty times to get out your vegan butter of choice. Most of these items you will use so frequently that it's best to go stock your fridge with them right now. Think of this as a shopping list.

Vegan Butter: Find a brand of vegan butter you like, such as Earth Balance. The options are typically made from blended oils and usually come in tubs or sticks and are usually chillin' wherever the tofu hangs out in the refrigerated section of your grocery store. Be sure to scrutinize labels to avoid lactose-free or cholesterol-free options that are not vegan. Some even contain fish oil.

Vegan Egg Replacement: The vegan egg options are actually quite vast. You can use a boxed brand you trust (I made all these recipes with Ener-G Egg Replacer) or make a quick replacement yourself using either tapioca flour or flax seed meal.

Vegan Cream Cheese and Sour Cream: All dairy replacements are not made the same, and they don't all taste the same, so experiment until you find the right one for you. Try Tofutti brand.

Cooking Oil: For a standard cooking oil, I use grapeseed oil. It has a high smoke point, which makes it a good substitute for olive or vegetable oils. It's also high in unsaturated fats and vitamin E. Other good high-heat cooking oils are safflower oil and canola oil. However, be wary of canola—it comes from the rapeseed, which are often genetically modified (GMO).

Extra-Virgin Olive Oil: EVOO isn't a good cooking oil, because once it heats beyond the smoke point, the fat oxidizes and isn't good for human consumption. I use it only for dressings and for drizzling after cooking.

Salt: Salt should only have one ingredient: salt. Unless you're using a flavored salt, there should be no other ingredient listed on the label. I use sea salt because it's the purest kind.

Fruits and Vegetables: Organic, organic, organic. I only use organic because again, back to the simple approach: if you start with good quality produce, you have a better chance of a good quality meal. Going organic not only takes a large chunk of chemicals out of your diet, but you often have superior tasting goods, which means less work later on. So yes, it does make a difference. The extra money is worth it.

Vegan Cheese: If it's just some shreds, take your pick. As of now, there are only two brands that make a good vegan cheese that melts: Daiya and Follow Your Heart Vegan Gourmet. If you want to go the artisan vegan cheese route but can't find any in your local store, I recommend you dabble in your own cheese-making. Interested? Check out the book Artisan Vegan Cheese by Miyoko Schinner. It's a good one.

Non-Dairy Milk: For cooking, it's best to use unsweetened, unflavored non-dairy milks. I usually use either soy or almond milk. You can use whichever you prefer, although if it's a heavier recipe, I often go with almond as it has more natural fats, à la whole milk. If I don't specify which type of non-dairy milk to use, then you can pick between the two.

Alright, now that we've given you a rundown of what you can expect to find in this book, let's get on with it!

Recipe icons

The recipes feature icons (in the form of capital letter abbreviations) to indicate certain characteristics that may be of special interest to you if you are avoiding gluten or soy. They are as follows:

GF - Gluten Free: These recipes are inherently gluten free, either because all the ingredients are gluten free or there is a choice between two items in the ingredients list, the first one being gluten free. Otherwise, the recipe itself needs no alterations or substitutions.

SF - Soy Free: These recipes are inherently soy free, either because all the ingredients are soy-free or there is a choice between two items in the ingredients list, the first one being soy free. Otherwise, the recipe itself needs no alterations or substitutions.

GFO - Gluten-Free Option: These recipes need some ingredient substitution and cooking alteration to make them gluten free, but the information you need is provided in the headnote of the recipe.

SFO - Soy-Free Option: These recipes need some ingredient substitution and, perhaps, cooking alteration to make them soy free, but the information you need is provided in the headnote of the recipe.

1. THE MORNING AFTER

"Love is blind. And sometimes deaf and dumb."

This is the most important thing you will read in this book: Regardless of your food politics, take warning. ***Do Not Try to Convert Your Partner.*** Attempting to bring them over to your side—whatever side that might be—will be detrimental to your relationship, and will possibly make you look like a dick. Even if it works, they may resent you, and they will probably (definitely) gorge themselves on break-up chicken wings if things don't work out, just to spite you.

Originally we planned to put this note in the intro chapter. But then we realized many people skip the intro because they're seeking the instant gratification that Chapter One promises. This note is so important, we just didn't want to risk it being glossed over in favor of the sexier, more alluring Chapter One.

Even if you're not overtly attempting to change your partner, you should also avoid doing that thing where you secretly hope they will change "on their own." Many vegans enter veg-fusion relationships hoping that one day their love interest will make the switch "independently." We're housing "on their own" and "independently" in obnoxious quotations because in reality, most people who get into relationships hoping their partners will change also indulge in some sort of persuasion. This is what we call the "vegucation" style of vegan-on-omni dating, a guerrilla-esque method of conversion. It goes like this: seduce an omni, hook them, demand they eat your seitan sammy, and—bam—they are vegan.

DATING SOMEONE WITH THE HOPE THAT THEY WILL ONE DAY CHANGE IS ILLOGICAL.

Okay, it's not always such an aggressive approach. Sometimes it's more like a semi-unintentional slow-prod, or a sideways crabwalk into conversion. A plant-muncher starts dating an omni, engages them in thought-provoking conversations about veganism, crosses their fingers, and secretly hopes for vegan osmosis to occur. This seems innocent enough—all you're doing is educating them, right? Wrong. There's a fine line between educating and lecturing. Your views are yours, your passions are yours, and like Ayindé always says, you can take a horse to water but you can't hold their head under. It's totally illegal.

Dating someone with the hope they will one day change is illogical. Say it with us:

I can never change the person I am with. I should not expect my partner to change because I want them to. The only person I can change is myself.

ZOË: So if you shouldn't try and convert your partner, then what should you do? Let's talk for a minute about soul mates. Wait, wait, don't close the book—I don't mean soul mates in the "one person for everyone" sense. What I am referring to is finding another person who has a spirit and energy that mirrors and matches your own. This applies just as much to your friendships as it does to your romantic connections. It also applies to animals. I'm pretty sure my cat and I are kindred spirits—we are both really fickle and like to sleep on the radiator.

Don't look for someone you think you can convert one day. Instead, focus on finding a person who is right for you in as many facets as possible. If their level of compassion truly reflects your own, then they might (might, I said!) be curious about your lifestyle, excited to learn, and eager to try it

on. But they have to want it for themselves. Be their muse, not their dictator. No one likes a dictator. So, get that "if only they were vegan" dream out of your head. Look for someone who appeals to you as is. Cataloguing possible improvements will only lead to disappointment, and again, it kinda makes you look like a dick.

Remember: You can't bully someone into thinking your way is the right way. And why would you want to? So you can have some vegan arm candy? If it's not their own idea, they will probably resent you. (Remember the post-breakup wing binge.)

So for starters, focus on finding someone you truly connect with.

What it means to make a connection

ZOË: I've gotten a lot of shit for being a vegan who is open to dating omnivores. An iEatGrass.com troll, er, commenter, even called me a "vegan whore" once. According to him, engaging in some non-vegan P in V is akin to "stabbing animals in the back." I wrote him off as seriously sexually frustrated, but really, am I a bad vegan? Am I sleeping with the enemy? Maybe—but you might too if you saw what the enemy was packing in his boxers. Just kidding. I'm not that shallow. (Maybe a little.)

In reality, the reason I don't cringe when a date does dairy is this: being vegan doesn't guarantee compatibility, and more importantly, it doesn't guarantee a connection. Do I want someone to share my love for tempeh Reubens and fuzzy-headed baby chicks? Sure. But I also want someone who "gets me," who is supportive, passionate, driven, smart, funny, attentive, caring, and—of course—sexy as f*ck. And what if I find that person and, shit, he also likes to cook up a steak on his George Foreman? Then what? I write them off?

When I stew over my own relationships, the thought of missing out on past so-in-love-my-face-is-numb situations because my man eats meat is laughable. Scoffable, even. While veganism is an important lifestyle choice for me, what I value in a partner above all else is a real connection. The type of connection that has you talking like you've known each other for years. A connection that has all of your friends thinking you've joined a cult or moved to rural North Carolina to have a baby in secret, because they haven't seen you in months—you've been in bed the whole time with your new beau, listening to Cat Power and marinating in each other's juices.

You can't help who you're attracted to: vegan, omni, your brother's new girlfriend, your third cousin (eek!). This is a truth that has caused problems for millions—I mean, who hasn't listened to Jessie's Girl? Rick Springfield knows what's up. Attraction extends beyond aligning lifestyles, and this connection is where the vegan-on-omni dating dilemma is rooted.

Vegans make up a scant percent of the population, so the majority of the people you meet in the wild are not vegan. If you're solely searching for a vegan mate (what the veg world calls a "veg-

ansexual"), then you have to eliminate nearly everyone you come across organically from the potential partner pool. This is difficult, and what's more difficult is making a connection with someone, and then telling those butterflies in your belly to calm the f*ck down because this newcomer eats meat.

To complicate matters further, meeting another vegan doesn't automatically cue the church bells. Even when your lifestyles do seem to align, there is no guarantee you will like them. They could be obnoxious or boring or a religious zealot. But just for fun, suppose you do like them. They're everything you've ever hoped for and more. They couldn't be more perfect if you made them up during a little solo fantasy session. Well, that's great, but it doesn't mean your feelings will be requited, or that you're going to be compatible.

Ahhh, compatibility. While I have met many kind, caring vegans, I have also met some real judgmental asshats. Being vegan doesn't automatically make you immune from douchebaggery or ensure you're a terrific fit for every other vegan that waltzes through the door. We are not a 'one size fits all' type of pre-packaged deal.

Vegan or not, I want someone who is accepting of me—from my smoothest of moments to my most erratic behavior, my Friday night ensemble to my Saturday morning breath, and my love for animals, the environment, and my body. They don't need to drink my vegan Kool-Aid—although I promise it's tasty. If they accept and support my choices, then that's enough. Why? Because our connection goes beyond my veganism!

Before I talk myself in circles, let's get to know each other better. And what better way to get to know each other than talking about our exes! That's what girls really do in public bathrooms, in case any men out there were wondering. We talk about our exes, and deconstruct the theory of relativity.

Ayindé: How I met my ex

You know Zoë, it's funny—that's what most guys talk about as well, their last relationship. That and, of course, socio-political inequalities in the developing world. But anyway, I'll start. I met my Ex, Ginger*, at the Moth. You know that event you probably heard about on NPR where people get up and tell stories? Yes, that one. So picture a crisp fall evening in SOHO. I was working as the executive chef at a popular café/restaurant in Union Square. I had just gotten off my shift and needed to blow off some steam. Yes, I blow off steam with red wine and watching strange people telling spoken word-ish stories.

By the time I got there someone was yelling that everyone from basically me to the back of the line wrapping around the corner wouldn't get in. So I snuck in by cutting the line. I figured no one would stop me if I furrowed my brow and looked like an ABM (angry black man). To avoid any

ATTRACTION EXTENDS BEYOND ALIGNING LIFESTYLES, AND THIS CONNECTION IS WHERE THE VEGAN-ON-OMNI DATING DILEMMA IS ROOTED.

noise from tattletales, I quickly took the closest empty seat which happened to be next to Ginger. I tapped her on the shoulder—she was in the middle of talking to her girls—and asked if the spot was taken. She gave me the "oh really, that's your line?" look, rolled her eyes, said "no," and turned her back to me. I was all like "whatevs, I'm just trying to sit, don't nobody want to talk to you!" Except she was pretty and had a big booty, and a nice smile. There is a song about this, right?

She was giving me the cold shoulder, and to make things more awkward, we were two of five black people in the building so everyone just assumed we came together. Luckily, at some point during the night, she warmed up to me. I would later learn that her friend Wendy had encouraged her to "stop being a B and talk to him, he's cute!" Thanks, Wendy!

Ginger's opening line was "So are you going to get up there and perform?" Um no, I said, I'm just here to watch; it's actually my first time. Ginger responded with "Oh, no? Hmm, you look like the type." I asked her to explain what the "type" was, and she sort of looked me up and down and said, "You live in Brooklyn right?" Yes, I did! I guess she took my regular uniform of jeans and a T-shirt and nappy 'fro to mean I was ready to start dropping prose in staccato.

By this point, I could see she was a pistol. Just my type. Before the night was over, we had a couple more bantered exchanges. I told her I was a chef, and she mentioned she was an executive. I commented on how young she looked for an executive. "I guess I'm a young executive." Touché. Later, while bundling up at the door in preparation for the cold NYC night air, Wendy piped up again, "So you're a chef, do you know where we can go get some good soup?" I started to think aloud, "Well there's Cafeteria..." Ginger cut me off with "We'll find something, I'm sure. You have my number, so use it. Have a good night." Again, ain't nobody trying to go get soup with you, girl! Bye!

Following the rules of dating, I didn't call her for a week. And when I did, she pretended not to remember me. Nice try.

Me: "It's Ayindé, the chef, the vegan chef."
Ginger: "Ohhh. Hi."

We chatted for awhile and tried to set up a date, but she was out of town with her job for most of the next two weeks, so we ended up just having more phone calls and this old-school "oh look, it's been two hours" phone conversation courtship. Finally we managed to set up a date. We met at a restaurant in Brooklyn, and she ordered the burger, medium. I had the edamame and fries. Then she asked the question.

Her: "So you're like vegan vegan, huh?"
Me: "Yep."
Her: "Wow."

This first-date conversation is par for the course for me. I can almost read my answers from a script. Yes (I'm vegan), no (I don't know what steak tastes like), yes (all my life), yes (that means no butter), no (I don't cheat), yes (I've been curious but not that curious). Ginger mentioned she was raised vegetarian, so she sort of knew about the lifestyle, but ended up going the opposite way.

"Why limit yourself?" she asked.

Her job included entertaining clients and she had no time to cook at the crib. We were polar opposites. She was loving what New York is known for: over 20,000 restaurants. She had her list of places that were best for meetings, breakfast, lunch, drinks, dinner, date nights, and late night spots. I, on the other hand, knew all the vegan hole-in-the-wall spots like the Punjabi spot all the cabbies go to on the LES (Lower East Side—cabbies know all the dope spots) or the $2.50 falafel in the village. And going out to breakfast seems crazy, partly because I can never find better pancakes than I can make myself.

You have to understand that at this point in my life, I really only had short-term relationships in mind. For one thing, I lived in NYC, and there really is no reason to date only one person for more than the winter. Coupled with the fact that I had not met a vegan or vegetarian woman that I was THAT attracted to (or an omnivore for that matter), and my thinking was, "I'll give it three months."

But Ginger was a bit more aggressive. We had a couple of dates between her hopping out of town for business. One night, on our third date or so, we met for drinks—which we did partly to take the veganism off the table, so to speak. We had a few extra drinks that night, and in the cab afterwards I leaned in for the cheek kiss and she kissed me on the mouth! Awww, yeah! The cab was parked outside my house, and I understood the look she was giving me and invited her up. And so it began— the most definitive relationship I'd had thus far.

Zoë: How I met my ex

I met Daniel* my freshman year of college. We were sitting on the same bench outside of our shared dorm. He was clipping his toenails. I was smoking a cigarette (I know, I know! Ahhh, youth). Anyway, years later, while pillow-talking, we found out that at the exact moment of introduction, we were both secretly thinking one another was disgusting. If mutual disgust doesn't spell romance, then I don't know what does. But really, who clips their toenails in public?

Later that year, the toe-clipping year, we ended up circling in the same group of friends. I was dating this guy who would only eat bacon and tuna salad. Obviously, that wasn't going to last, and so after I broke up with Tuna, I started eyeing Dan. And flirting with Dan. And showing up at places I knew he was hanging out...like his dorm room.

Eventually, after several weeks of minor league stalking, everyone knew I liked Daniel. Everyone except for Daniel, that is. A shy, quiet guy by nature, Dan was showing absolutely no special interest in me. Of course, this made me like him even more. Later, over more pillow talk, I found out Dan didn't know I was interested in him, despite the fact that all of our friends—male and female—were onto me. I'm not sure what was up with our friends. Aren't dudes supposed to let other dudes know when a girl is into them? Isn't it like man code or something?

AREN'T DUDES
SUPPOSED TO LET OTHER DUDES know
WHEN A GIRL IS INTO THEM?

As Dan had no idea I was into him, you can imagine his surprise when, after several double shots of Burnett's coconut vodka, chugged out of a shot glass emblazoned with the slogan "Size Matters," (remember, youth!), I worked up the courage to make my move. A group of us were hanging out at the campus pizza place, and so my roommate stood guard as I stealthily followed Dan into the men's bathroom.

By this point, I hope a few things are clear: (1) this is obviously a love story to withstand the tests of time; and (2) I can be sort of predatory when it comes to dating. I also tend to draw from my friend pool often.

F*ck the friend zone. I do what I want. I actually think dating your friends is the best way to go. Most of my serious relationships bloomed from deep friendships. Think of it this way: If you date someone you were friends with first, you have probably already peeked into their psyche. Maybe you've even met their family. You know they're not completely crazy. Or maybe you know that they are, and that's what you like about them. While a new side of them will emerge once you remove each other's clothes, you have at least an inkling of what you're getting into. You've seen the way they treat their partners. You know how they take their coffee and what music and hobbies they're into. They won't horrify you by telling you three weeks in that they're "not really a cat person" or invite you to join them on an Ayahuasca spirit journey. Also, if someone has watched me act batshit crazy during previous breakups, and still want to date me, well then they must be a keeper.

If the feelings are brewing, and the sexual tension is present, breaking out of the friend zone is sort of like sliding through an unlocked back door instead of drunkenly hunting for your keys at the front. It's a bit more graceful. Of course, there's always that risk of it going bad and ruining your friendship. But all of the best things in life are the riskiest, are they not? I mean, that's the only reason unprotected sex is still a thing. It's dangerous, but damn if it doesn't feel good. (Public Service Announcement: wear condoms!)

Oh right, back to Dan. So I followed him into that bathroom, my roomie holding it down outside to block any intruders. Upon closing the door behind me, I momentarily blacked out. I regret never knowing what classy way I managed to confess my feelings to Daniel, but I am sure it went something like, "I want to make out."

When I came to, I was perched on the sink, my legs wrapped around Dan's waist, engaging in some PG-13 heavy petting. I didn't know how I got from the door to the sink, but I was happy that things seemed to be going well. Unfortunately, our story-book moment was ruined when a drunken junior managed to evade my roommate, stumbled into the bathroom, and immediately began vomiting. In between wretches, he kept turning to Dan and uttering a very convincing and pitiful, "I'm so sorry, dude. Just keep going, I'm so sorry."

And so our relationship began.

Dan was not a vegan. He was not even a vegetarian. He was, however, a happy, healthy eater. His excitement to try everything, whether it was a burger or tempeh teriyaki, put a buffer between our opposing lifestyles. Eating was one of the myriad reasons why things didn't work out with Tuna. We were so different from one another; even killer foreplay couldn't distract me from our juxtapositions. Well, not for too long, anyway.

So let's say you've met someone new, and in many ways, they are different from you. You have lifestyles that may not exactly align—in fact, some of your views may even directly oppose one another. But you like them, you seem to click, and the sexual connection is f*ck-me-sideways insane.

Unfortunately, butterflies in your tummy or a killer sexual connection are not reason enough to keep a relationship going. If they were, we'd all be marrying those one night stands from college. Sometimes your differences—and the way you handle them—are going to cancel out your passion party. I call these differences "deal-breakers."

*Smallprint: Names in this book have been changed to avoid immense assholery. Daniel once confessed his anxiety over what I might write about him on the Internet. He said nothing, however, about what I might write in print! See, it pays to be specific...

In the upcoming chapters, we will be giving you a plethora of tips for making your relationship work from every angle. But before you've got a toothbrush at their place and maybe a shared pet or—for those of us scared of commitment and responsibility—shared small kitchen appliances, we want to help you spot a situation in which your differences may be a deal-breaker. Maybe you've only been on one date. Maybe you're already fuggling (that's snuggling with an F). But before it goes any further, stop filling your Pinterest boards with fantasy wedding ideas and think hard about whether or not your differences are going to make your relationship impossible in the long run.

If you believe in one thing, and your other believes in, well, another thing, then shit can get messy. Check out the following section for a handful of tips that can help you tell if your opposing beliefs are deal-breakers.

How to Spot a Deal Breaker

ZOË: **How big are your differences?** You know what I'm gonna say: size matters. At least, it certainly does when it comes to your differences. Opposites attract all the time, and heated debates can be incredibly sexy. But when it comes to major lifestyle choices, you need to take a step back, break away from whatever pheromones you're drunk on, and consider these questions:

- Are your differences manageable, or do they cause conflict on a daily basis?

- Do they make you incompatible?

- Will they get in the way of any future you may have together? (Sorry to freak your freak, commitment-phobes.)

Say you're a vegan activist, and you just met a hunting fanatic. You spend all your time volunteering for Farm Sanctuary while they spend hours at Cabela's. This is a difference that will certainly rear its ugly head and wreak havoc on anything you're trying to build together. But maybe you're an omnivore who just met a hottie behind the counter at that local juice bar. They are all hopped up on kale and have six rescued pit-bulls. Yes, your bacon habit may be an eye-roller for them, but this difference is a bit more manageable. It may take separate pots and pans, but I wouldn't throw in the relationship towel just yet.

AYINDÉ: **Can you trust them?** Trust is a tricky thing. It's what's implied when you say "I love you" to each other for the first time; you really mean "I trust you not to be a dick about my heart, okay?" "Yes, I will not be a dick with your heart" is how "I love you too" roughly translates. Trust, like love, is an action. So, can you trust that the person you're with respects your choices and is not going to slip a pat of butter in your green beans 'cause it's easier than making two separate sides?

ZOË: **Can you communicate?** This is huge, and is important to pay attention to in the beginning of a new relationship. When you talk about your differences, does it cause a big blow-out fight? If you can each calmly state your opinions, respect each other's opposing beliefs, and maybe even learn something, then this is a good sign.

However, if you're screaming about animal husbandry while your boyfriend tells you to stop acting like an insane person because "one burger isn't hurting anybody," this will be a major issue, especially if it leads to you shoving the issue under a rug. Not talking about a problem doesn't mean the problem doesn't exist, and you can't ignore those elephants forever. Eventually they will surface, and no matter how steamy the make-up sex is, having the same argument over and over without an ability to see eye-to-eye will not lead you to relationship bliss. This is why I had to swear off dating Leos back in 2008. Stubborn-on-stubborn makes a big ole sloppy mess.

AYINDÉ: Are they willing to grow? My parents have been married for forty years, throughout which they have grown a lot. They went from sharing cartons of cigarettes to creating vegan babies and a mini-vegan empire. Why? Because they were willing to try new things—things that were good for them, their family, and the planet. If your potential partner is not willing to grow with you, making changes can be hard. They don't necessarily have to be willing to make changes themselves, but they do have to be willing to support your changes. No support at home makes everything hard, especially changing the way you eat.

TRUST, LIKE LOVE, IS AN ACTION.

ZOË. Are you willing to compromise? I know I really like someone when I am willing to compromise. If you're not willing to give in order to take, then your differences are probably a deal-breaker. As a vegan, if you would never allow animal products in your home, then you can't expect to build a future with someone who wants to eat animal products and doesn't ever want to live in a meat-free space.

You never know how things will work out. Sure, maybe they will get so moved by a showing Food Inc. that they will eschew meat and dairy forever, and you will live in domestic vegan heaven for the rest of your days. But being with someone while hoping they will change isn't healthy or honest, and you need to face reality: continuing with the relationship means you expect the other to change while at the same time remain unwilling to compromise on your end. Move on and find someone who either fits your bill, or for whom you are so gooey-faced that you will reconsider your stance just a little bit. (A little bit I said! Stop stink-eyeing me.)

AYINDÉ I have a great story about compromise, but I'll get into that in Chapter 6. For now, it's time to eat.

The Breakfast Recipes

Meals to share, fresh out of the sheets

Breakfast is one of my favorite meals to make. You can make a decadent breakfast on a lazy Sunday, or do it quick and easy after a long night of vigorous...er, debate. And when it comes to impressing the opposite sex, breakfast is a clear winner. Any old shlub knows that cooking dinner for a date is romantic, but you, you're going to take it a step further by making a huge stack of Orange Cream Stuffed French Toast (page 33) for your bed buddy first thing in the morning. Not only does it ensure that they stick around at least long enough to eat it, but it's the easiest way to seal the deal with a "damn, and he can cook?" Or maybe it's "damn, at least he can cook" depending on the ole bedroom skills, or lack thereof. No judgment.

There's an old saying in Catholicism: "Only two people know you're having sex. God and the neighbors." If you didn't get a "Can you keep your love-making to a minimum?" knock-back from the guy next door, you can try to make up for it with a killer breakfast presentation...

Lover's Hash

Prep time: 5 minutes | Cook time: 20 minutes | Serves 2 to 4 | SF, GF

I came up with this hash whilst in Hawaii with Zoë. We were having a working breakfast during the production of a feature film Zoë wrote that I was acting in. It was a "make what we have in the kitchen" kind of day, and luckily, what we had in the kitchen was really working. The composition of this recipe is excellent. Red potatoes are best as they will not turn to mush when you cook them. Kabocha squash (Asian pumpkin) is my top choice for the squash, but if you can't find it, acorn squash will do. The squash will cook faster than the potato, so be sure to follow the instructions!

3 tablespoons grapeseed or safflower oil

2 cups diced red potatoes

1 cup diced kabocha squash

1/2 cup diced onion

2 cloves garlic, minced

1 small bell pepper, stemmed, seeded, and diced

2 teaspoons dried basil

2 teaspoons dried rosemary

1/2 teaspoon salt

Black pepper

1. Heat the oil in a large skillet over medium-high heat, until hot and shimmering. Add the potatoes. Cover and cook for about 10 minutes.

2. Add the squash, the rest of the veggies, and the herbs. Cook, uncovered, for about 10 minutes. Mix well. Make sure the onions are soft and well cooked.

3. Reduce the heat to low, cover, and cook for about 10 minutes longer, mixing with a spatula from the bottom until the potatoes and squash are fork tender. Add the salt and pepper to taste. Eat the hash on its own or as a side to another favorite breakfast dish. I suggest the Spinach and Mushroom Quiche, coming at you on page 36.

Watermelon Mimosa

Prep time: 3 minutes | Serves 2 | GF, SF

Who doesn't love an excuse to booze at breakfast? This recipe happened out of nowhere. I had an overripe watermelon and some champagne lying around. I added some fresh mint and POW. Refreshing morning drunkenness. Please POW responsibly.

1 cup cubed seedless watermelon

1 tablespoon fresh lime juice

2 teaspoons chopped fresh mint

1 bottle chilled champagne

1. Combine the watermelon, lime juice, and mint in a blender and blend until smooth.

2. Using a sieve, strain out and discard the pulp.

3. Fill a juice glass halfway with the watermelon blend and top with cold champagne.

Andouille Sausage and Biscuits

Prep time: 5 minutes | Cook time: 20 minutes | Serves 2 to 4

As I was saying, I am a sweet 'n' savory kinda guy, and this is one of my favorite quick morning eats. You can prep the sausage a day or two in advance, and the biscuits are pretty quick as well. They can also be made in advance and frozen, then defrosted when you need them.

BISCUITS

1 cup all-purpose flour

1/2 tablespoon baking powder

1/2 teaspoon sea salt

4 tablespoons vegan butter, very cold

1/2 cup unsweetened almond milk

SAUSAGE

3/4 cup Lightlife Gimme Lean vegan
　　sausage (see Note)

1 tablespoon Cajun seasoning

2 teaspoons paprika

1 teaspoon minced garlic

1/2 teaspoon freshly ground black pepper

1/4 teaspoon sea salt

1/4 teaspoon gumbo filé powder

1/4 teaspoon chili powder

1/4 teaspoon red pepper flakes

1/4 teaspoon ground cumin

Grapeseed or safflower oil

1/2 cup julienned green bell pepper

1/2 cup julienned red onion

1/2 cup vegan cheese shreds

OPTIONAL TOPPINGS

Vegan butter

Raspberry jam (or you favorite flavor)

1. **Biscuits:** Preheat the oven to 425°F. In a medium bowl, mix together the flour, baking powder, and salt. Using a fork, mix in the cold butter until the butter becomes the size of small peas. Slowly add milk, gradually stirring until the dough pulls away from the side of the bowl.

2. Place the dough onto a floured surface, and knead 15 to 20 times. Pat or roll dough out to a 1-inch thickness. Cut the biscuits with a large cookie cutter or the top of a juice glass dipped in flour. Repeat until all the dough is used. Brush off the excess flour, and place the biscuits onto a lightly floured baking sheet. Bake for 13 to 15 minutes, or until the edges begin to brown.

3. **Sausage:** In a large bowl, break up the sausage. Add the Cajun seasoning, paprika, minced garlic, black pepper salt, filé powder, chili powder, red pepper flakes, and cumin. Mix well. Take 1/4 cup of the sausage mixture and form into a 1/2 inch thick patty. Repeat until all patties are formed. It should make approximately 4 patties.

4. In a large skillet over medium high heat, heat 1/4 cup of the oil until hot and shimmering. Fry the patties for 3 to 5 minutes on each side until golden brown. Transfer the patties to paper towels to cool. Reserve the oil in the skillet.

5. Reheat the skillet with the oil from the sausage over medium heat. Add the bell pepper and onion and sauté until caramelized, 5 to 7 minutes. Use a spatula to push the onions and peppers into four piles large enough to cover the sausage patties and sprinkle the top of each veggie pile with 2 tablespoons of cheese, allowing it to melt. Using a spatula, place the vegetables and melted cheese on top of each sausage patty. Serve with hot biscuits on the side, or make some sammies and watch that expression of "awww" pass over your partner's face as they realize you can cook! Feels good, doesn't it?

NOTE: I use the Lightlife Gimme Lean brand vegan sausage because it sticks together well, allowing you to add flavor and still turn it into patties. It took some super scientific research to figure out that this is the best brand to use for this recipe. And by "super scientific research," I mean throwing sixteen pounds of the "wrong" kind in the trash and having to get the "right" kind two hours before our Lusty Vegan Comedy Show event in Brooklyn in 2012. So yeah, it's worth it to hunt down that particular brand.

WTF is gumbo filé powder? Gumbo filé powder is made from dried sassafras and is necessary for any authentic Creole or Cajun recipe. If you can't find it in your regular grocery store, check out a specialty spice store, or order it online. If you really can't rustle it up (it's not that hard to find, trust), then a quick substitute for that earthy flavor is ground dried sage in an equal amount.

Cloud 9 Pancakes

Prep time: 5 minutes | Cook time: 10 minutes | Serves 2 to 4 | SFO

"Why do most vegan recipes have to be so complicated? I can't get a simple stack of pancakes when I want them? I mean, is it so hard to make a breakfast staple without buckwheat and banana? Where is the baking powder? I mean I want to enjoy my breakfast too! I have needs!" At this point in my rant, I would be standing and—according to Ginger—shouting. I don't think I was shouting, just firmly stating my opinion that it's hard to find a simple, traditional, fluffy vegan pancake recipe out there that doesn't taste...you know..."healthy." So I made my own. This is the best vegan pancake recipe you will ever make. You deserve it. To make this soy free, use soy-free Earth Balance.

1 1/2 cups all-purpose flour

2 tablespoons cornstarch

1/4 teaspoon sea salt

1 1/2 tablespoons baking powder

1 tablespoon sugar

Egg replacement mixture (see below)

1 cup almond milk

2 teaspoons vanilla extract

3 tablespoons vegan butter, melted

Maple syrup and vegan butter, for topping

Pro-Tip: The key to great pancakes is heating the skillet or griddle to a true medium-high. Watch for air bubbles on the surface of the batter, and this lets you know that they are halfway done.

1. In a medium bowl, combine the flour, cornstarch, salt, baking powder, and sugar. In a small bowl, make the egg replacer and combine it with the almond milk and vanilla. Using a whisk, combine the wet and dry ingredients and mix gently until combined. You want some lumps. Gently fold in the melted butter and mix. Make sure the batter is still lumpy and thick.

2. Heat a griddle or skillet over medium-high heat and coat lightly with oil. A spray-on oil works best to avoid over-oiling. Use a dry measuring cup to pour 1/4 cup of batter in a circle. Cook until the surface of the pancake has small bubbles all around, 3 to 5 minutes, then flip. Ideally you should only have to flip once.

3. On your serving plate, stack the pancakes high to seem impressive, or, as Darth Vader would say, "most impressive." Top with butter and maple syrup and voilà! Pancake ninja.

HOW TO MAKE A VEGAN EGG REPLACER

3 tablespoons water

1 tablespoon Ener-G Egg Replacer

Pour the water into a small pot and bring it to a slow simmer. Slowly add the egg replacer and whisk vigorously for 1 to 2 minutes, then remove from the heat and set aside for about 1 minute. The consistency should be think and gelatinous. One batch equals one egg. If the recipe calls for 2 eggs, then double it, and so on. It's ok to add a bit more water if it gets too gummy.

(The Closest I'll Ever Come To)
"Chicken" and Waffles

Prep time: 10 minutes | Cook time: 30 minutes | Serves 2 | GF

If you haven't been to a pop-up food event, they're pretty cool. Basically, a chef (that would be me) comes to a space to cook for a short period of time, be it a day, a weekend, or a week. One of these events was a waffle brunch series in Brooklyn held every Sunday for a few months, called Petit Déjeuner. A vegan waffle brunch series—I mean, can you get any more Brooklyn than that? This was my favorite of my many hustles. Brooklynites loved it. I made some cash, coupled it with catering gigs and well, that was my life. As I write this, I honestly don't remember how I made it work, and Ginger definitely didn't see how it could work. She had never dated an entrepreneur. The point is, I knew I could make it work eventually, and I did. And I came up with bangin' gluten-free waffles in the meantime. You're welcome.

TEMPEH

2 tablespoons safflower oil

4 ounces tempeh, cut in 1/4-inch cubes

1/2 cup diced onion

3 cloves garlic, minced

1 teaspoon dried sage

1/2 teaspoon red pepper flakes

1/2 teaspoon dried basil

1/2 teaspoon dried thyme

1/4 cup low-sodium wheat-free tamari

1/4 cup water

WAFFLES

1/2 cup all-purpose gluten-free flour

1/2 cup chickpea flour

1/4 cup almond meal (see sidebar)

2 teaspoons baking powder

1 1/4 teaspoons xanthan gum

1 tablespoon cane sugar

1/2 teaspoon sea salt

1/4 cup vegan butter, melted

1 1/4 cups almond milk

1 teaspoon vanilla extract

1. **Tempeh:** Heat the oil in a medium skillet over medium-high heat, until hot and shimmering. Add the tempeh and fry until golden brown on all sides, 5 to 7 minutes. Add the onions, garlic, sage, red pepper, basil, and thyme. Sauté until the onions are translucent, about 5 minutes. Add the tamari and water. Cover with a lid, reduce the heat to medium-low, and allow the tempeh to braise for 7 to 10 minutes, stirring occasionally. The liquid will reduce and the tempeh should have flavor throughout. Remove the tempeh from heat and set aside.

2. **Waffles:** In a medium bowl, combine the dry ingredients and mix well. Add the milk, vanilla and melted butter and mix well with a whisk. Your batter should be on the thick side.

3. Coat a hot waffle iron lightly with spray-on oil. Using a dry measuring cup, pour 1/2 to 3/4 cup of batter evenly onto the iron. Close the waffle iron and cook until steam stops coming out of the sides, 3 to 5 minutes. Transfer the waffles to a plate, pile on the tempeh, top with some syrup, and enjoy.

WTF is almond meal? Almond meal is easily made from blanched ground almonds. If you don't have time for that, you can also buy it by the bag or in bulk in most health food stores. Want to DIY? Use the interwebs to hunt down the technique.

Lemon Meringue Chia Pudding

Prep time: 5 minutes plus 2 days | Serves 2 | GF

I discovered chia seeds in 2011. I was looking for a new dessert to add to one of my menus for my "Wildflower Weekend" pop-up. I ended up making a cardamom spiced pudding. However, I wanted to take it step further and make a cross between a yogurt and pudding. What would you call that? A yodding? A pugurt? I think it's all in how you say it. Just elongate the u sound and use a French accent. Puugurrrtt. See? Fancy.

1 cup almond milk

1 cup raw cashews, soaked in water
    overnight and drained

1 teaspoon lemon zest

2 tablespoons fresh lemon juice

2 tablespoons agave nectar

Pinch of salt

3 tablespoons chia seeds

1 ripe melon (for plating, optional)

1. Combine all of the ingredients except the chia seeds (and melon) in a blender. Blend the mixture on the high setting until smooth. Taste and adjust lemon or sweetener to your liking.

2. Whisk the chia seeds into the mixture (make sure they don't clump up).

3. Pour the mixture into a glass jar. Cover with a lid and refrigerate overnight, or at least 2 to 10 hours to allow the chia to form the pudding.

Pro-Tip: Remember we eat with our eyes first, so here is a plating trick to help your cause. To plate your pudding, take a ripe melon and cut it in half. Spoon out the seeds and scoop the pudding into the middle. Serve cold with a spoon. Forgot to get a melon or just don't feel like being fancy? Then f*ck the melon and eat the pudding straight from the jar. We won't judge.

Note: Soaking your nuts (ha!) allows your body to digest them easier, which ups their nutritional value, but more importantly for this recipe, it alters the texture. A soaked cashew is undeniably creamier than an unsoaked one. So, soak away, preferably for 8 to 12 hours.

"Feed them great food. They can't say shit when their mouth is full." – KATE,
VEGAN

Orange Cream Stuffed French Toast

Prep time: 35 minutes| Cook time: 5 minutes | Serves 2

I developed this next recipe while I was in NYC in my first few months as an executive chef. I immediately launched a brunch menu. Soul Music Sunday Brunch quickly became the most popular day we had at the restaurant. It was a "thing," which is why the music thing was a BIG deal. While I came up with more than a few goodies, this was a staff favorite and is one of those dishes that make you curse (as in *damn* that's good!) before you realize it. When you pair it with a couple of things we've already made—like the Andouille sausage and the hash recipe that's coming up next—well, the mouth orgasms multiply. If that's not how you like to spend your Saturday (or Tuesday) mornings, well then we probably can't be friends. This recipe does take a bit of technique to make, so I suggest starting off right with a sharp knife and great bread. Note: The bread makes the meal, so go ahead and splurge on the good stuff.

1/2 (1 pound) loaf unsliced French bread

FILLING

1 cup (8 ounces) vegan cream cheese

1 tablespoon sugar

1 teaspoon orange zest

1 tablespoon orange juice

1/2 teaspoon vanilla extract

1/4 teaspoon orange extract (optional)

1/2 teaspoon salt

BATTER

1 cup almond milk

1 cup raw cashews, soaked in water overnight and drained

2 teaspoons vanilla extract

1/2 teaspoon salt

FINISHING

Grapeseed or safflower oil, for frying

Vegan butter

Pure maple syrup

Fresh blueberries

1. Using a sharp knife, cut the bread into thick slices. Next, cut a slit in the side of the bread slices so they're partially open, like a pocket. Be careful not to cut all the way through. Set aside.

2. Filling: In a small bowl, combine the cream cheese, sugar, orange zest, orange juice, vanilla, orange extract (if using), and salt. Whisk until smooth. The mixture should be thick and slightly sweet. Transfer the filling mixture to a piping bag or use a spoon to fill the bread pockets with the filling mixture. Set aside.

3. Batter: In a blender, combine all of the batter ingredients and blend until completely smooth. Pour the batter into a large shallow baking dish. Add the stuffed bread and soak on both sides for about 20 minutes (or up to 30 minutes for a richer flavor). You want the bread completely soaked.

4. Coat a large skillet or griddle with oil and heat over medium-high heat. Carefully place the French toast in the hot skillet. Cook until golden brown on both sides, about 3 minutes per side. Serve topped with vegan butter, maple syrup, and blueberries.

WTF is a piping bag, and do I need one? Piping bags are easily found in the baking section of some stores. If any of you Pinteresters want to DIY, just take a zip lock bag and cut the bottom corner off, making an opening the size of a chopstick bottom. Boom.

Grits Risotto

Prep time: 5 minutes | Cook time: 20 minutes | Serves 2 | GF

This recipe was inspired by my experience with risotto. I never really got to enjoy risotto because of the heavy cheese factor in most risotto dishes. However, grits have had a place in my home since I was little. The thick and creamy consistency of the really good grits can be analogous with risotto, so in this mash-up dish, I replaced the mouth feel of the starchy rice with corn grits and kept the creaminess of the grits to come up with this. It's a great savory morning breakfast food, which was good, because Ginger liked savory food in the morning. I, on the other hand, prefer sweet stuff in the morning, so I was catering to Ginger with this one.

VEGETABLES

1 tablespoon grapeseed or safflower oil

1/2 cup chopped red onion

1 tablespoon chopped garlic

1 tablespoon chopped fresh basil

1 tablespoon vegan butter

1/2 cup sliced shiitake mushrooms

GRITS

2 cups water

1/2 cup white corn grits

1/2 cup unsweetened soy milk

2 tablespoons vegan parmesan

Sea salt

1 tablespoon black truffle oil

1. Vegetables: Heat the oil in a medium skillet over medium-high heat. Add the onion and sauté for approximately 3 minutes, until lightly browned. Add the garlic and sauté for an additional minute. Add the basil and sauté until slightly wilted. Remove from the heat.

2. Heat the butter in a separate skillet over medium high-heat until melted. Add the mushrooms and sauté for 4 to 6 minutes. The mushrooms will absorb the butter, so add a little more if you think it needs it. Cook until golden brown, then remove from heat.

3. Grits: Bring the water to a boil in a medium saucepan over high heat. Whisk in the grits and reduce the heat to medium-low, whisking continuously. Once the grits start to thicken, reduce the heat to low, stir in the milk, mix well, and cover.

4. Add the sautéed vegetables and parmesan to the grits, whisking until well incorporated. Salt to taste, remove from the heat, and serve immediately. Garnish the grits with the reserved mushrooms and black truffle oil.

"I am vegan living with an omni. He respects me, and I respect him, even though I don't agree with his omni ways. I cook for myself, and he cooks for himself. Simple. I do wish he would become vegan, and maybe one day he will." – TERESA, VEGAN

No-Tofu Spinach and Mushroom Quiche

Prep time: 60 minutes | Cook time: 40 minutes | Serves 4 | SFO

Yes, a quiche. I made this during one of my challenge phases. Every now and then I challenge my-self to veganize something that traditionally is not vegan. So basically anything with egg I tried and failed, and tried again. Finally I remembered a chef I worked for used chickpea flour for an eggy consis-tency. And now you get to reap the benefit. Do you know how many kitchen ninja points you will score from have a homemade quiche laying around? A gazillion. However, like many awe-inducing recipes, it's a project, and it has to set for a while after you make it, so prepare yourself. Like all vegan custard-based recipes, this takes practice. Luckily, quiche is an "eat anytime" food, so pop one in the fridge for all-week eating. To make this soy-free, use a soy-free vegan butter and vegan Worcestershire sauce. You can cut the prep time in half if you use a storebought crust.

1 unbaked 9-inch vegan pie crust, storebought or make your own (as follows):

HOMEMADE PASTRY DOUGH

2 cups all-purpose flour

1 1/2 tablespoons sugar

1 teaspoon salt

3/4 cup cold vegan butter

6 to 9 tablespoons ice water

QUICHE FILLING

1 tablespoon vegan butter

1 tablespoon safflower or grapeseed oil

1 cup chopped red onion

1 cup chopped red bell pepper

1 1/2 cups thinly sliced mushrooms

1 teaspoon minced garlic

1 teaspoon dried thyme

1 teaspoon dried rosemary

1 tablespoon minced fresh sage

1/4 teaspoon salt

1 (5-ounce) bag fresh spinach, chopped

Egg replacement mixture for 1 egg (page 27)

1 cup chickpea flour

2 1/2 cups water

1 teaspoon ground turmeric

2 teaspoons vegan Worcestershire sauce

1/2 teaspoon onion powder

1/2 teaspoon garlic powder

1 tablespoon nutritional yeast

1 teaspoon salt

3/4 teaspoon black salt (I use Kala Namak)

1/4 teaspoon red pepper flakes (optional)

1/4 teaspoon freshly ground black pepper

1 tablespoon melted vegan butter, for brushing

1. **If making homemade pastry dough:** In a medium bowl, combine the flour, sugar, and salt. Using a large fork or a pastry blender, cut the butter into the flour. Working quickly, lightly rub the flour and butter through your fingertips until the mixture is like crumbly sand.

2. Start mixing the dough gently with a wooden spoon as you add cold ice water, 1 tablespoon at a time. Add water until the mixture becomes a firm yet crumbly ball. Wrap this ball in plastic wrap and refrigerate for 60 minutes. Remove the ball 15 minutes before you are ready to roll it into your pie/quiche pan. Roll the ball to about 1/8 inch thick and line the pan with dough. Trim off any overhang. Set aside or refrigerate until needed.

3. You just made your own pie crust. I hope you feel really good about yourself. You should probably take a picture of it and share it with all of your social networks, and don't forget to hashtag #TLV. Now before your ego gets so solid you could bake that and eat it, let's move on to the challenge of the quiche custard.

4. Quiche filling: Melt the butter in a medium skillet over medium-high heat. Add the onions and mushrooms and sauté for 3 minutes. Add garlic, thyme, rosemary, sage, and salt and sauté for 2 minutes longer. Reduce the heat to medium. Add the spinach and salt and sauté until the spinach wilts. Remove from the heat. Preheat the oven to 350°F.

5. In a medium saucepan, bring 1 1/2 cups of water to a boil. Add all egg mixture ingredients except the chickpea flour and salt.

6. In a separate bowl, combine chickpea flour and remaining cup of water. Whisk well to combine. Once the water is boiling, slowly add the chickpea-water mixture. As you mix, it will become very thick. Reduce the heat to medium and continue to cook for 2 to 3 minutes, stirring constantly, until thick and glossy. Remove from the heat and add the reserved vegetable mixture. Mix well and add the remaining salt to taste. Spread the filling evenly into the prepared pie crust. Smooth the top with a spatula and bake for 20 minutes.

7. Remove the quiche from the oven and brush the top with melted butter and bake for an additional 5 minutes. Allow to cool to room temperature before serving. This is the hardest part of being a chef: the wait. I know, it's really hard, but it will be so much better if you let it cool first!

Pro-Tip: Kala Namak is a specific kind of salt originating in India. It will lend the dish an eggy, sulfur-like flavor.

Stories from the Field

Latham Thomas, Founder of Mama Glow

"I don't need to share a similar diet and lifestyle to find common beliefs. I'm always looking for what brings people together in my work and certainly in my relationships. Our connection is far beyond the fork; it's celestial.

My top tip for vegans looking for love is to follow your heart. Explore the hidden dimensions of your soul. Seek to open yourself completely. Tell the truth, and be vulnerable. Don't believe what you see—believe what you feel. Seek to make each other better. Bring your best self to the relationship. You want to be with an amazing person—become that amazing person, and your divine reflection will appear before you."

"This is for the omnivores. It's spelled seitan, not satan."

You're not a vegan. And let's face it: you may never call yourself a vegan. I mean, you like vegetables alright. The potato is a vegetable, right? But you also love a good buttery croissant, and what would life be like without the occasional drunken grilled-cheese binge? That nut cheese just does not "taste like the real thing." Also, you think the phrase "nut cheese" is just gross.

You've got a lil' hottie who loves sprouts and kale, but you love medium-rare steak. Despite this, you come back for more, so you are open-minded! Congratulations. But take heed: against our good advice, the kale-muncher you are sleeping with may be waiting to "convert" you, artfully plotting to seduce you, turn you into a vegan, and then leave you crying in your quinoa as they start the cycle over with another poor, unsuspecting omni, creating a whole new league of vegans!

No, not really. However, if they haven't read the super important note in Chapter 1 ("Never Try to Convert Your Partner"), then they may be secretly hoping that you one day jump aboard the veg bus. It's nice in here. We have vinyl seats and free cocktails.

The reality is, once it's past the fun hook-up-on-a-Friday-night phase, and past the awkward "soooo, what are we?" phase, and into the comfy "we" are an "us" phase, then it's time to know how to handle your vegan.

With infatuation comes a willingness to try new things. You hit some vegan-friendly restaurants and order the zucchini Alfredo with bean balls. Heck, even enjoy it! (Of course you do, vegan food is delicious.) But eventually you realize that this person might be the one. Like, really "the one." You realize that you don't want them to go anywhere, and that—unlike the six months you only wore black and idolized Marilyn Manson—their veganism is not a "phase." While you eventually stopped listening to The Dope Show on repeat, they may never start eating meat. So maybe it's time to really understand what veganism is all about, so that the two of you can coexist in omni-on-vegan harmony.

FOOD IS EMOTIONAL AS WELL AS SENTIMENTAL.

The closest comparison to this divide is dating someone who supports a different political party than you. No, scratch that—it's more like dating someone of a different religion, because there is guilt involved. One minute you're walking down the street, hand in hand, love in your eyes, and the next you're

fighting about the idea that you can still have nice shoes if they're not leather. "Yes, even though they don't keep my feet dry, I'm doing it for the cows!" says your vegan. "Yes, the point of shoes is dry feet, but there is another point!" Things can get that weird.

AYINDÉ: If I met someone, we fell in love, and then one day she told me I had to start eating pork rinds and ribs if I wanted to be with her, I would delete her number so fast, she'd think she was on one of those old MTV dating shows. I'm not really into double standards. Okay, that's not true, some are good, but what I'm saying is I don't expect you, O Omnivorous One, to go vegan for your partner. (You can breathe now.)

Food is emotional and sentimental. Think about all of the BBQs your dad cooked in the summer, all the fried chicken and cornbread stuffing with lots of butter your mom made on special occasions, the s'mores you ate at camp, the In-N-Out burger you have every time you're in LA. Think of all the tastes you've acquired as an adult, and imagine quitting them cold turkey 'cause your partner says

if you don't, they won't love you anymore. In some circles, that kind of controlling attitude might be considered bat-shit crazy. At the very least, it's an "unreasonable request." How do I know? I've made it. Yep, I asked Ginger to change her life for me. She said...well, let me get back on track.

At some point, I felt like Ginger could be "the one" with an asterisk. If I could only make her vegan, then she'd be perfect. I know what you're thinking: "But Ayindé, everyone knows women are in charge in relationships." And someone can't be "the one" with stipulations. Love should be unconditional! Well, my friend, nobody told me that at the time, and ignorance was sheer bliss.

Ginger, the aforementioned pistol, was more rooted in her convictions than a lil' romance, good dick, and fried tofu could excavate.

Ginger and I watched the "Oprah Goes Vegan" episode. Now, I was trying really hard to use discretion upon my viewing, as Oprah suggested. I'm a very empathic person, so when I see pain, I feel pain. I didn't want her to know this just yet. It's not because I didn't care about the topic or was afraid to show emotion in front of a lady. Clearly, I care a lot. When people—regardless of what their diet is like—are faced with the barbaric practices of the modern meat industry, they usually are affected in some way, and I wanted to gauge Ginger's reaction without letting too much of my own show. In other words, it was a test.

I think that the only way to change a person's way of living is with a fundamental shift in how that person thinks. You need to have a reaction before you take action. If you don't think anything is wrong with killing to eat, if you can wring a chicken's neck, feather it, fry it up, and put it on the table—if you have no issue buying meat without thinking about where it came from, then you most likely will not change unless you have some kind of fundamental shift in consciousness. The conviction has to be strong, because change is really f*cking hard. I knew this, and so when we watched this episode, I was looking for her to have an "aha" moment. Instead, I had one.

I was raised by vegan parents, and so I was brought up with a really different outlook than most Americans. My opinion is that you can live and eat your way through this life and cut out the middle mammals. Instead of fattening up cows, pigs, and chickens with grains, we can eat those grains ourselves, and use them to feed millions of starving people, the same way ancient civilizations did. To me—someone with no emotional connection to meat whatsoever—this is a viable option, not only beneficial for all animals (humans included) but for the longevity of our earth. Now to be clear, that is my opinion, but it happens to be shared with a few experts and world leaders, and millions of vegans, so whatevs. It's hard to be humble when you have science AND history on your side.

Now, my vegan ego had quite a shock post-Oprah segment when Ginger said, in response to factory farming, "I mean, it's gross how they do it, but what's a cow doing with his life anyway? Besides being delicious?"

She lol'd. I blank stared. Like her name, Ginger could be very, ummm, punchy. While she may have been trying to get a rise out of me (and she did) it was truly what she thought. That was the "aha" moment for me, and looking back, I only remember the emotions, not the actual he said/she said.

I was all sorts of verklempt, while she seemingly carried on with her signature "bad stuff happens, nothing you can do about it so why bother?" attitude. I say "seemingly" because I always leave room for misinterpretation. I am, after all, human.

But I digress. It was her opinion, it was real, and it was the first real time I noticed how real her realness was. We had a fundamentally different view on how we went about life, and we both felt strongly about it.

But the thing was, even with opposing strong feelings, I still felt very strongly about her. It's interesting when someone comes along and makes you realize just how much you believe in what you proclaim. Veganism had always been a part of me, literally since birth. I never questioned it, I believed in it blindly, it made sense to me, and so I didn't ask why. I am sure that's how most omnis operate, too. You were born with beliefs, you developed emotions around an attachment to them, and it takes a whole lot to rock those loose.

But Ginger, she was making me BE the man I said I was. She was sharpening my point of view. She would ask questions like "Why? Why is it so important to you? Everybody eats meat, and they are fine. Just have small piece of steak and veggies. It's balanced, and you don't have to be vegan just because you were raised as one."

To a person who has only known veganism, I had to begin to make my choice, not because my family chose it for me, but because we live in a time where you can literally choose your own adventure. Now, I wasn't changing. I like this ride, and I hop on it every day. But it took Ginger and what we were building to show me that I was, in fact, choosing it.

ZOË: Luckily for me, Dan was cool with my veganism. He was very environmentally conscious—

sometimes to a fault. I once had a meltdown in a supermarket as he rattled off reasons why the coffee I chose was murdering our commerce system (it wasn't fair-trade). Oh, and don't get me started on the flack I got from riding on a jet ski one summer (polluting the ocean), or the noise I heard when I bought a knock-off pleather bag from China Town (supporting terrorism). Wait, wait. Back it up. I'm supposed to be ruminating over the sweet moments! Because Daniel was really very sweet.

One evening, our romance still in the fledgling stage, we were returning from dinner in Dan's beat-up old Saturn. After I got out of the car, he told me to wait a minute. Popping the trunk, he removed a small blue cooler. Surprise! A post-dinner treat. He had made me vegan chocolate mousse.

In actuality, it was more like vegan chocolate milk. The texture was adorably wrong. Instead of thick and rich, it was thin and drippy. But the fact that Dan had researched a recipe and then got down to brewing up a batch of vegan mousse in his college townhouse—shared with five beer-guzzling dudes who were probably making fun of him the whole time—really puddled me up.

I ate (drank) it all, truly touched, trying not to think about Dan's disgusting kitchen, moldy pizza boxes piled by the door, and floors still sticky from last weekend's kegger. I imagined what his roommates were saying about him while he worked. "Dude, did you see what he was putting in that blender?! Tofu and, what? Cacao!? Man I hope he gets laid." He did.

That wasn't the only time Daniel's sweetness took me off guard. On our one-year anniversary, he planned an elaborate scavenger hunt for the two of us by filling a basket with slips of paper and asking me to reach in and pick one. Each paper had a place around campus that was sentimental to our relationship, like that bathroom we first drunkenly tongued in, or a bench we shared a memorable snuggle on, the tennis court where he tried and failed to teach me to play, and the small dock by our sewage-infested college lake where we had our first al fresco tryst. I would pick a slip of paper, read its contents, and then we would head off to visit that place in a scrap-book style adventure mission in celebration of our first year together. It was very genuine, and endearing, and if I didn't love him before that, I definitely loved him after. You see, Dan had a knack for forethought and planning, and a little of that goes a long way, I tell you.

Tips for Omnivores

With Dan's skills in mind, here are some tips for you, the omnivore, on making your lettuce hound happy without having to ditch dairy yourself.

Do research

The first thing you should do when you find out someone you're dating is vegan is learn what the lifestyle is all about. This way, the next time you talk about it, you won't irritate them with questions like, "So you don't eat dairy? What about cheese? Eggs? Fish? Fish aren't really animals..." We know they say ignorance is bliss, but in reality ignorance is only blissful for the ignorant. Everyone else will think you're an ass.

Talk about it

After you've done your research and can successfully pronounce quinoa and know what "nooch" is (psst: it's vegan slang for nutritional yeast), bring up your partner's veganism on your own. This will make you look thoughtful and caring. Also, your partner may be a bit nervous talking about it in your new relationship for fear of coming off as preachy. And if they do end up being a bit preachy, well, bite your tongue and come at it with an open mind. Find out what camp your little vegan falls into. Are they a super-cool pop vegan? An environmental stud? Pro-PETA? Knowing this will help you maneuver through future scenarios.

Be open-minded

If you're down to date a vegan, then you've won half the battle. Good for you. As you push forward, you will learn all sorts of cool things, like what kind of underwear your new bae prefers and what the f*ck spirulina is. The key to connecting with your vegan—or at least avoiding many a public argument—is keeping an open mind and trying new things when they should arise. No one will judge you if you don't like hijiki salad, but you should at least try it. Good food is good food, whether it's vegan or macrobiotic or raw. If it's prepared well, it will probably be tasty, so give it a shot before you wrinkle your little omni nose. This open-minded attitude should not stop at mealtime. Your vegan probably has myriad opinions about their concern of choice: animal rights, the environment, the industrialization of our country's food system, essential fatty acids, what foods are necessary to sculpt Herculean abs, any and all of the above. Listen, engage, and add your own flavor to the conversation. Look at you, being all mature and progressive!

Stock up on meat-free eats

Before you get your panties (boxers? briefs? however you accessorize down there!) all up in a bunch, mind you, we're not suggesting you stop eating meat. We will never ask that of you, I promise. However, if you're far enough into your relationship where you're camping out at each other's places, then you might want to pepper your pad with some vegan staples. Please don't stock your freezer with Boca burgers and call it quits. I mean, you bought this book so you could learn how to cook for your honey-free honey, right? I know you can't have the ingredients for beer-battered tempeh tacos on hand all the time, but at least stock up on a few go-tos:

- Fresh veggies will never go uneaten with a vegan in the house
- Non-dairy milk for that morning coffee will always be appreciated
- Hummus is an unofficial food group in the eyes of many grass munchers
- Say it with us: Peanut. Butter. (Try to go organic or at least "all natural." The only ingredients in a good peanut butter are peanuts, and maybe a wee bit of salt.)

Make an effort.

It never hurts to make an effort to show someone you like the way they're put together. Remember Daniel and the mousse? Show your little foodie some affection so they can feel like the star of a quirky Zooey Deschanel rom-com where everyone is impeccably dressed and eating marinated tempeh in the park. No? Just me? Whatever. Some simpler ideas that don't involve storing chocolate mousse in a mini-cooler in the trunk of your car:

- The most obvious foodie romance tip is getting all of the ingredients for a fancy-shmancy meal, and suggesting you cook it together. However, if your cooking skills are seriously lacking, then just ask them to teach you how to cook a vegan dish. Instead of doling out the "Oh, I'd cook for you, but I can't cook vegan" line or pretending to help when all you really do is wash the tomatoes and ogle their butt, ask your vegan to give you a little kitchen tutorial. This is a way to turn the whole "I can't cook" situation into a cute opportunity to accidentally rub up against each other as you crowd around the stove.

- If you want to eat out, you don't have to go to an all-veg place. Depending on your location, there may not even be an all veg place around! No sweat. Just research the menu of a restaurant before suggesting it—trust us when we say that no vegan walks into a restaurant without first scrutinizing the menu online and no, we don't just want to order a salad. You will seem really sweet when you say, "Hey, let's check out Olives and Sauce, because I hear they have some great vegan options." Swoon!

- Is it lovely outside? Go for a picnic! I really do like that marinated tempeh in the park idea...I wasn't joking!

- Have a food-tasting party. Instead of one large meal, make a ton of appetizers. This way, you can try all sorts of vegan-friendly dishes, work on your plant-based cooking skills, and have an excuse to eat with your fingers. Just don't feed each other like total drips. Unless you do it Lady and the Tramp style. Yeah, okay, maybe don't do that either.

Perfect a few recipes

All of the recipes in this book can be used to impress your vegan babe. Just picture it: they're standing in your kitchen, stomach a-rumbling. They suggest you order in, and you say "Why order in, when I can whip you up my specialty of <insert appealing-sounding vegan dish here>?" Their eyes will light up, and their pants will come off. Okay, well, maybe not in exact succession, but you smell what we're stepping in. Get a few recipes down hard so that you have confidence in your ability to make them, and make them well. We know what you're thinking. "But, Zoë and Ayindé, I don't know shit about vegan cooking! Can't I just boil up some noodles?" No, you can't! Well, not if you want to be impressive—and we know you want to be impressive. That's why you're reading this here book, remember?

For learning how to manhandle a simple vegan staple, we suggest you pay close attention to Chapter 7, "Five Things to Do With Tofu." Tofu is a stereotypical vegan favorite, second only to the dastardly kale. But it is, in fact, a favorite of most cruciferous creatures, so make it your biff. We suggest perfecting the Mexican Lasagna or Ayindé's Fried Tofu—so good, he named it after himself. But we digress. Enjoy the following recipes, for they are sure to please and impress your vegan mate.

Recipes to Impress Your Vegan

It's time to warm up the oven

"Make a veggie stir fry big enough for two and pull out half for a perfect vegan meal while the Significant Other adds meats. I don't believe in trying to change other people, so I'd never make someone eat what I eat if they don't want to. However, if the other person is open minded and wants to try vegan food, then why not make something for them? Cooking together is a great way to bond as a couple and strengthen a relationship." – LINDSAY, VEGAN

Jambalaya

Prep time: 10 minutes | Cook time: 40 minutes | Serves 4

I came up with this recipe as the centerpiece for a spread in *Essence Magazine*. They asked me to come up with several different meal ideas. The process was nerve-wracking because when you're put on the spot, it's easy to forget all you know. But I gathered my wits and relied on what I liked: flavorful, filling, and maybe a little indulgent. This meal was accompanied by Bananas Foster and a Caesar salad.

2 tablespoons vegan butter

3/4 cup chopped green bell pepper

3/4 cup chopped onion

3/4 cup chopped celery

1 tablespoon chili powder

1 tablespoon ground sage

1 1/2 teaspoons red pepper flakes (reduce for less heat)

1 teaspoon ground thyme

1/4 teaspoon cayenne pepper (optional)

2 cloves garlic, minced

2 medium tomatoes, cored, seeded, and chopped

3 bay leaves

1 (15-ounce) can red kidney beans, rinsed and drained

2 tablespoons vegan Worcestershire sauce

3/4 cup dry brown rice

8 ounces vegan sausage links, sliced in rounds

4 ounces seitan, chopped

1/4 cup grapeseed or safflower oil

2 tablespoons salt-free Cajun seasoning

Sea salt

1. In a large skillet over medium-high heat, melt the butter. Add the bell pepper, onion, and celery and sauté for approximately 5 minutes.

2. Add the chili powder, sage, red pepper flakes, thyme, cayenne (if using), garlic, tomatoes, bay leaves, beans, and Worcestershire sauce. Stir in the rice and slowly add 3 cups of water. Reduce heat to medium, cover, and cook until rice absorbs water and is tender, stirring occasionally, about 35 minutes.

3. In a medium bowl, combine the sausage, seitan, oil, and Cajun seasoning. Mix well to coat. Once rice is almost done, add the sausage mixture to the skillet and mix well. Add salt to taste.

4. Cover and cook for another 5 minutes. Serve hot.

Shiitake Bolognese
with Zucchini Fettuccine

Prep time: 5 minutes | Cook time: 35 minutes | Serves 2 | GF

Zucchini makes a great pasta substitute, but what's pasta without a great sauce? *Nothing!* Shiitake mushrooms and tofu make a great Bolognese with a hearty, meaty texture. Combine them with onions, carrots, and red wine, and you have created a Tuscan experience that will satisfy both the vegan and the omni at the table.

4 medium zucchini

2 tablespoons grapeseed or safflower oil

1/2 cup organic extra-firm tofu, drained
  and crumbled

1/2 cup diced tempeh bacon

1/2 cup chopped onion

1/2 cup chopped celery

1/2 cup grated carrot

1 teaspoon minced garlic

2 cups sliced shiitake mushrooms

1 cup water

1 (6-ounce) can tomato paste

1 cup red wine

1 cup cherry tomatoes, sliced

1 teaspoon fresh thyme

1 teaspoon dried basil

1 teaspoon dried oregano

2 tablespoons nutritional yeast

2 tablespoons olive oil

2 teaspoons cane sugar (or agave nectar)

1/2 teaspoon salt (more to taste)

1. Using a potato peeler, peel all the outer green skin from zucchini. Using the peeler, shave noodle-sized strips from top to bottom, rotating the zucchini as you go, stopping when you get to the zucchini's seed center. Place the zucchini noodles in bowl, cover with cold water and add 1/2 teaspoon of salt. Set noodles aside and drain when ready to serve. Don't allow the noodles to soak longer than an hour.

2. In a saucepan over medium heat, heat the oil until hot and shimmering. Add the tofu and cook for 8 to 10 minutes, stirring with a spatula from the bottom occasionally to prevent sticking. Add the tempeh bacon, onion, celery, and carrot and sauté for 5 minutes. Add the garlic and mushrooms and sauté for 1 minute.

3. In separate bowl, combine the water and tomato paste. Mix until smooth. Add the red wine to the veggie sauté and let the alcohol cook off, 2 to 4 minutes. Add the tomato paste mixture, cherry tomatoes, and herbs. Reduce the heat to medium-low. Add the nutritional yeast. Keep at a low simmer for approximately 20 minutes, stirring occasionally. Add the olive oil, sugar, and salt. Remove from the heat. Serve over the zucchini noodles. The hot sauce and cool noodles create a fresh burst of flavor and texture. In yo mouth!

"It may seem obvious, but read the damned ingredients before you offer your vegan girlfriend a snack...I've made that mistake too many times." – Pietre,
OMNIVORE

Loaded Quinoa Nachos

Prep time: 20 Minutes | Cook time: 10 minutes | Serves 2 to 4 | GFO

I served these nachos at a Super Bowl pop-up in Brooklyn in 2012, when the Giants won the game. After the game, the subways were a riot over the win, but during the game, the restaurant was a riot over my quinoa nachos. Use gluten-free flour to make this gluten-free (and check the ingredients on your vegan Worcestershire sauce – if it contains wheat, use more tamari instead.)

QUINOA MIXTURE

1 cup quinoa, well rinsed

2 tablespoons grapeseed or safflower oil

1/2 cup diced onion

3 garlic cloves, minced

2 tablespoons dried sage

1 tablespoon dried thyme

1 teaspoon dried oregano

1 teaspoon red pepper flakes

1 tablespoon chili powder

1 tablespoon ground cumin

2 tablespoons low-sodium wheat-free tamari

2 tablespoons vegan Worcestershire Sauce

Salt

CHEESE SAUCE

2 tablespoons vegan butter

2 tablespoons all-purpose flour

2 cups unsweetened soy milk

2 1/2 cups Daiya cheddar cheese shreds

1/2 cup nutritional yeast

NACHOS

1 bag tortilla chips of choice

2 to 3 scallions, chopped

1 (4-ounce) can black olives, sliced

1 jar chunky salsa

OPTIONAL TOPPINGS

Guacamole

Refried beans

1. Quinoa: Bring 2 cups of water to a boil in a small saucepan. Add the rinsed quinoa and reduce the heat to medium-low. Cover and cook until the water evaporates and the quinoa is cooked to a fluffy texture, approximately 15 minutes. Set aside.

2. Heat the oil in a large skillet over medium-high heat. Add the onion and sauté until they become translucent, 3 to 5 minutes.

3. Add garlic, sage, thyme, oregano, red pepper flakes, chili powder, and cumin and mix well.

4. Add cooked quinoa to the skillet, along with the tamari and Worcestershire sauce, and mix well. Reduce the heat to medium-low and cook for 5 to 7 minutes. Add salt to taste.

5. Cheese Sauce: In a medium saucepot over medium-high heat, melt the butter. Add the flour and whisk to blend. Reduce the heat to medium and cook, stirring to brown the mixture for 1 to 2 minutes.

6. Whisk in the soy milk and bring to a boil. Stir in the cheese and nutritional yeast and cook, stirring constantly to melt the cheese. Once the cheese is melted, remove the pot from the heat and set aside.

7. Assembly: To assemble the nachos, make a bed of tortilla chips on a large serving dish or plate, cover with warm quinoa filling, and top with cheese sauce, green onions, olives, and salsa. Add guacamole and/or refried beans, if using. Serve hot.

Mung Bean Tostadas

Prep time: 5 Minutes | Cook time: 40 minutes | Serves 2 to 4 | GF, SF

I discovered mung beans when working as an executive chef in New York. My sous chef brought me a Kitchari recipe and after trying it out, it became a favorite. Mung beans resurfaced with me while I was on tour with India.Arie because of her strict diet. She was craving Mexican food but couldn't eat pinto beans, so I thought, what else could I use? Mung beans—EUREKA! We had tostadas. Mung beans are gluten-free, full of fiber, and have the same mouthfeel as refried beans.

Note: If you can only find sprouted mung beans, remember that will reduce the cooking time by 7 to 10 minutes. If you use them, watch your beans closely.

2 cups water, or more

1/2 cup dry mung beans

1 tablespoon ground cumin

2 teaspoons chili powder

1/2 teaspoon smoked paprika

1 teaspoon nutritional yeast

1 teaspoon sea salt (more to taste)

2 teaspoon olive oil

4 corn tostada shells

TOPPINGS

1/4 cup chopped purple onion

1/2 cup chopped Roma tomatoes

2 cups shredded romaine lettuce

2 pickled jalapeños, chopped

Salsa

1 avocado, pitted, peeled, and sliced

2 limes, cut in quarters

1. Bring the water to a boil in a medium saucepan. Add the mung beans, cover, and lower the heat to medium-high. Cook for 10 minutes, then lower the heat to medium-low. Continue to cook until the water begins to evaporate and the beans split open, 35 to 40 minutes. At this point the texture of the mung beans will become similar to refried beans. When the beans break down, they will have a powdery taste, but when they're almost done cooking, that taste goes away. You made need to add more water, 1/2 cup at a time.

2. Once the desired consistency is reached, add the cumin, chili powder, and smoked paprika, stirring well to mix the ingredients together. Add the nutritional yeast and olive oil. Remove from the heat.

3. Place a tostada shell on a plate and top with 1/4 cup of the mung beans. Add the toppings of your choice. Boom!

5 Things You Didn't Know About Mung Beans

1. They are rich in soluble dietary fiber, which helps lower cholesterol

2. They contain protease inhibitors, preventing breast cancer

3. They're a low-glycemic food, which means they are diabetic friendly

4. They have more than 3 grams of protein per serving

5. They are a good source of phytoestrogens, helping to regulate hormonal activity

Kung Pao Tempeh

Prep time: 30 minutes | Cook time: 7 Minutes | Serves 2 | GF

One Sunday night, to satisfy a Chinese craving, Ginger suggested I make Kung Pao. She was a big fan of what I came up with, and said it was a great signature dish because it was a double entendre for my cooking style, like kung POW!

TEMPEH

2 tablespoons grapeseed or safflower oil

1/2 (8-ounce) package tempeh, cut crosswise into 1/8-inch sticks

2 tablespoons Shaoxing wine or white wine

1 tablespoon low-sodium wheat-free tamari

1 tablespoon peanut oil

RICE

2 cups water

1 cup dry brown rice

SAUCE

2 tablespoons Shaoxing wine or white wine

1 tablespoon low-sodium wheat-free tamari

1 tablespoon rice vinegar

1 tablespoon chili paste

1 teaspoon brown sugar

2 tablespoons toasted sesame oil

1/4 cup chopped green onions, white and green parts

1 (8-ounce) can water chestnuts, drained and rinsed

1/2 cup roasted, unsalted peanuts, chopped

1 tablespoon minced garlic

2 tablespoons cornstarch

1/4 cup + 2 tablespoons water, divided

1. **Tempeh:** Heat the oil in a medium skillet over medium-high heat. Add the tempeh and cook until golden brown on all sides, 8 to 10 minutes total. Set aside. Combine the marinade ingredients in a glass dish, place the cooked tempeh in the marinade, and allow it to sit for 30 minutes, turning the pieces over halfway through. While the tempeh marinates, make the rice.

2. **Rice:** (See Pro-Tip below) In a small saucepan, combine 2 cups of water and 1 cup of rice and bring to a boil. Reduce the heat to low, cover, and cook until the rice is done, approximately 25 minutes. Remove from the heat.

3. **Sauce:** In a small bowl, whisk together the wine, tamari, rice vinegar, chili paste, brown sugar, and toasted sesame oil. Add the green onions, water chestnuts, garlic and peanuts. In a separate small bowl, combine the cornstarch and 2 tablespoons water and set aside.

4. Heat the sauce mixture in a medium saucepan over low heat, until it becomes aromatic, approximately 3 minutes. Remove the tempeh from the marinade and add the tempeh to the sauce, coating it completely. Add the reserved marinade to the tempeh mixture and increase the heat to medium. Once you get to a light simmer, add the cornstarch and water mixture. This will cause the liquid to thicken. Cook, stirring, for approximately 2 minutes. Add more water to make sauce more liquid if desired. Once the proper consistency is reached, remove from the heat and serve hot over the rice.

Pro-Tip for Bangin' Brown Rice: Not all rice is made equal. To start off right, clean the grains by running water over them until the water is no longer cloudy.

Tofu Sausage Pizza Sliders

Prep time: 10 minutes | Cook time: 15 minutes | Serves 2 to 4

Pizza is the easiest to make. You start with a dough or bread, add tomato sauce, a lil' vegan cheese and veggies and you have pizza. I personally love using English muffins for pizzas, because they're delicious but also the perfect size for appetizers, a game day snack, or a quick late-night nom-nom.

TOFU SAUSAGE

8 ounces extra-firm tofu, frozen and defrosted, loosely crumbled

2 tablespoons grapeseed or safflower oil

1/2 cup finely diced onion

1 teaspoon minced garlic

1 tablespoon chopped fresh rosemary

1 teaspoon dried basil

2 teaspoons dried oregano

1 teaspoon dried sage

1/4 teaspoon red pepper flakes

2 tablespoons low-sodium wheat-free tamari

1/4 cup water

1/4 teaspoon sea salt

PIZZA AND TOPPINGS

2 English muffins, sliced in half

1 (26-ounce) jar marinara sauce

1/2 cup diced bell pepper

1/4 cup diced onion

1 (8-ounce) package shredded Daiya Havarti-Style cheese

1. Tofu Sausage: Wrap the tofu in a clean kitchen towel and squeeze out excess water. In a medium skillet over medium heat, heat the oil until shimmering. Add the tofu and cook until brown and somewhat crispy, stirring from the bottom to prevent burning, 10 to 12 minutes. Add the onion and sauté until translucent, 2 to 3 minutes.

2. Add the garlic, rosemary, basil, oregano, sage, and red pepper flakes to the skillet, then stir in the tamari, water, and salt. The flavor should be pungent and a little salty. Add more herbs or salt, as desired. Remove from the flame and set aside. Preheat the oven to 350° F.

3. Pizzas: Arrange the sliced English muffins on a baking sheet. Spread 2 tablespoons of marinara sauce on each muffin. Top each muffin evenly with bell pepper, onion, the reserved sausage mixture, and cheese.

4. Arrange the pizzas on a baking sheet and bake for 10 to 15 minutes. Let cool for a few minutes before eating to avoid burning the roof of your mouth, and enjoy.

"It works if you do the work. Compromises are key, and flexibility."

– MEL, VEGAN

Beer-Battered Tempeh Tacos

Prep time: 40 Minutes | Cook time: 10 minutes | Serves 4 to 6

I was planning my Wildflower San Francisco pop-up for Cinco de Mayo back in 2013 and wanted to think of great street food ideas. Of course, fish tacos came up, and it looked like something I could easily recreate with tempeh. The beer batter makes a light, crunchy exterior, while the marinated tempeh inside adds complexity to this simple dish. The tangy sauce and cabbage round it out to make it a meal. The prep time includes the marinating step, so to make 'em faster, marinate the tempeh the night before.

TEMPEH

3/4 cup low-sodium wheat-free tamari

1/4 cup fresh lime juice

1 tablespoon dried basil

1 tablespoon dried oregano

1 tablespoon Old Bay seasoning

1 teaspoon dried thyme

1 pound tempeh, cut into 1/8-inch strips

SAUCE

1/2 cup plain vegan yogurt

1/2 cup vegan sour cream

2 tablespoons fresh lime juice

1 jalapeño chile, seeded, and minced

1/2 teaspoon ground cumin

1 tablespoon fresh dill

1/2 teaspoon sea salt

BATTER

1 cup all-purpose flour, plus more for dredging

2 tablespoons cornstarch

1 teaspoon baking powder

1/2 teaspoon salt

1/2 teaspoon black pepper

Egg replacement mixture for 1 egg (page 27)

1 1/2 cups beer (I use ale)

TACOS

1 1/2 cups safflower oil (for frying)

1 package (5-inch) corn tortillas

TOPPINGS

2 cups shredded green cabbage

1 small yellow onion, sliced

1. Tempeh: Combine the tamari and lime juice in a shallow bowl. Add the basil, oregano, Old Bay seasoning, and thyme and mix well. Add the tempeh to the marinade. Cover and set aside to marinate for 40 minutes.

2. Sauce: In a separate bowl, combine the yogurt and sour cream. Whisk in the lime juice until the sauce is runny. Stir in the jalapeño, cumin, dill, and salt. Set it in the fridge. When the tempeh is done marinating, remove it from the marinade with a slotted spoon and transfer to a plate. Place the plate with the drained tempeh close to the batter bowl, and have your cooking station close to the stove.

3. Combine the flour, cornstarch, baking powder, salt, and pepper in a bowl and mix well. In a separate bowl, whip up the egg replacer with water until frothy (1 1/2 teaspoons egg replacer, 3 tablespoons warm water). Working quickly, add the beer to the egg mixture and whisk gently to combine. A few lumps are okay.

4. Tacos: Over medium-high heat, heat the oil in a saucepan. Now is also a good time to warm your tortillas. Wrap them in foil and place them in the oven at 350°F. Dust the tempeh with the flour mixture, then dip it in the batter, coating completely. Immediately drop the battered tempeh into the hot oil. The tempeh will float to the top. Turn with tongs and cook until golden brown on both sides, 3 to 5 minutes. Once done, remove from the oil and drain in a bowl lined with paper towels. Repeat until all the tempeh is done.

5. Fill each warm tortilla with two pieces of tempeh, a handful of shredded cabbage, and some onion. Top with the white sauce.

Farmers Market Ratatouille

Prep time: 8 minutes | Cook time: 20 minutes | Serves 4 | GF, SF

When I was transitioning from New York City to LA, I visited my mom, pops, and sisters. My sister, Makini, VP of the family business and a Seattle celebrity chef and owner of Plum Bistro restaurant, had accidentally double-booked herself. She had a cooking demo at a local farmer's market that she couldn't do, so I told her I would fill in. But what would I cook? I recently saw the movie Ratatouille, and although the idea of a rat in the kitchen is disgusting, I liked the recipe idea. The market would have all the ingredients I needed. No rats were involved in the making of this recipe.

1/4 cup grapeseed or safflower oil, plus more as needed

1 1/2 cups diced yellow onion

1 teaspoon minced garlic

1/2 teaspoon fresh thyme leaves

2 tablespoon thinly sliced fresh basil leaves

1 cup diced green bell pepper

1 cup diced red bell pepper

1 cup diced zucchini squash

1 cup diced yellow squash

Salt

2 cups chopped hen-of-the-woods mushrooms (or chef's choice)

1 1/2 cups chopped tomatoes

1 tablespoon chopped fresh parsley leaves

Freshly ground white pepper

1. Heat the oil in a large skillet over medium heat. Once hot, add the onion and garlic and cook, stirring occasionally, until the onions are softened and lightly caramelized, 5 to 7 minutes.

2. Add the thyme, basil, green and red peppers, zucchini, and yellow squash to the pan. Sprinkle some salt on the mix and continue to cook for an additional 5 minutes.

3. Add the mushrooms, stirring occasionally, until they are tender, approximately 5 minutes.

4. Add the tomatoes and parsley, season with pepper to taste, and cook for a final 5 minutes. Stir well to blend and serve either hot or at room temperature. In order to keep the fresh flavor and texture of the vegetables, be careful not to overcook the mixture.

Bibimbap, page 140

"This one goes out to all the vegans..."

Here is a fun fact: over 60 percent of vegans have never seriously dated another vegan. Considering how passionate we are about this here movement, that is a shocking number, especially because 45 percent of us claim that finding a vegan partner is "very important." That means many of us are grappling with dating someone whose lifestyle differs from ours...or lying on vegan dating questionnaires. Dating is a social event, and that's what this chapter is all about—navigating the social arena of dating someone who is intrinsically different.

Being upfront with yourself about what you want will help weed out those who aren't right for you, before you waste time on second (and twelfth) dates. As we already went over in Chapter 1, you can't choose who you fall for, but you can ask yourself this question:

Can I love someone who eats animals? If the answer is no, then you may be dabbling in vegansexuality, and should move on ahead to Chapter Four. If the answer is yes, don't feel guilty or weird about it. Just know that like most things in life, it won't be easy.

When it comes to relationships, Yoda was wrong. There isn't only do. Trying is important as well. All relationships take effort, and when committing to someone whose values directly oppose yours, well, it takes even more effort. Sometimes you will triumph. Sometimes you will fail hard. But that doesn't mean you shouldn't try.

A vegan goes dating...

ZOË: Ahhh, dating. The most awkward of all recreational sports. When getting to know someone, most of us want to walk the fine line of accessibility and mystery. You want to let your personality shine through while simultaneously trying not to terrify anyone. I'll never forget the look on Daniel's face the time he stumbled on my copy of The Sexual Practices of Quodoushka. Gulp.

When your date isn't vegan (you can tell by the steak they just ordered...), you might wonder when it's appropriate to pepper the vegan informational nugget into conversation. Of course you want to stay honest and true to yourself, but if you're crushing on your date, you don't want to freak their freak too soon. Early dating banter usually covers career and hobbies and awkward yet weirdly unifying childhood stories, not deeply rooted philosophical beliefs. Hold out for a moment that seems organic to avoid sounding spastic.

Don't: "Should we start with drinks? The weather is super weird this week, right? I'm vegan!"

Do: Ask the waiter for the vegan options and let that be the conversation starter.

I'm not saying you should hide your veganism or be ashamed of it! Heck no. But you're just getting to know someone, so timing is important. I'm wary about chatting religion and politics on a first date, too.

Long before Daniel and I were exclusive, I went on this memorable date with a guy I met at a karaoke bar. It was our first date, and we went to this fancy Indian restaurant. I asked the waiter if

the samosas were vegan, and then my date and I started talking about my veganism. Excitedly, he told me that he doesn't eat dairy because it really activates his IBS. Not knocking IBS, and I do love a good potty joke, but really dude, on the first date? And while I'm eating? No more trolling for dates at karaoke night for this little lady...

AYINDÉ: Yes, first dates definitely tell the tale. I mean, what other black man orders the tofu option for no reason? Or what man in general, for that matter? I'm instantly outed as a vegan once those words exit my mouth. As Ginger and I got further into things, we began to merge our social groups, mainly by hanging out with her coupled-up friends. In the beginning, Ginger would let me pick the restaurant, but if we were out with a group, I would feel weird making everyone eat "my kind of food," and there were only about three spots in NYC where I would eat. So we basically stuck with ethnic restaurants like Ethiopian and Mexican. I don't think we ever went to a steak house or a French bistro. I like bread and salad as much as the next guy, but I'm not that kind of vegan who will march into a steak house and demand a full protein vegan option. My chef background gives me some professional courtesy.

Most omnis think veganism is "limiting." Your omni family, friends, and co-workers expect you to "cheat." If you're the type who approaches veganism as a lifestyle, and not a diet, then you probably don't cheat. I don't cheat at all, which can create awkward moments when I have to turn down a bite of something that's "soooo good." I'm sure it is. But "no thank you" he said, high-horsing-ly.

Ginger has a summer birthday, and it fell during our early months together. She booked a small resort in in the Poconos. We had a nice road trip, and that's when the lifestyle hiccups began to unfold—how I snack versus how she snacked, how it's hard to eat at pit stops, and no fast food guilty pleasures. Special occasions were another thing. At her birthday dinner, Ginger had a steak. Like a good omni girlfriend, she called ahead and made sure they had something for me; it was some sort of overly decorated pasta. Over dinner, she asked the second inevitable question: "So how do you handle traveling and stuff, if you can't eat?" Well, I go where I know I can eat. I'm never unprepared to cook something, or else I'm going to go hungry, and I don't just get hungry, I get hangry. And I try not to let that happen, so I just grab my nuts, my bag o' vegan nuts, that is. The point is, these questions—and the vegan's responses—are very defining. They come up eventually. It showed Ginger what she was getting into. But she shrugged it off, and so did I.

Tips for vegans dating omnis

Okay, so now that we've talked about first date etiquette, let's talk about a few things that can help juice up your relationship when you're beyond date numero uno but still in the earlyish phases.

Talk about it

ZOË: As you move past the anxiety-riddled first few dates, it's time to talk more about your rad lifestyle. Yes, rad. You're really getting to know each other now, so it's a good time to explain while you always have an emergency stash of almonds in your purse. While it's good to discuss what you do and do not eat, it's more important to talk about why. Some vegans would rather not get into the specifics for fear of starting an argument. Some of us get really heated over our food politics. But not me. Nope. Never. While it may be good to avoid heated food debates with semi-strangers in public (or around holiday tables), it's important to be up front with your Sig-O so they understand you.

If your date is into you, they will hopefully be into learning about this lifestyle you subscribe to, even if they don't want to sign up themselves. When discussing your veganism, you can gauge their interest by their participation in the conversation. Are they asking questions? Or are they eyeballing their phone while you talk about the terrors of fox farming. I mean, who the eff wears fox fur anymore? What is this, 1922? Whatever, the point is to make sure you're acknowledged and understood.

WHILE IT'S GOOD TO DISCUSS WHAT YOU DO AND DO NOT EAT,
IT'S MORE IMPORTANT TO TALK ABOUT WHY.

About six months into our relationship, I overheard Daniel defending my veganism to a mutual friend who didn't "get it." Daniel calmly and clearly repeated a few eerily familiar-sounding lines about the depressing state of our country's agricultural system, the politics of eating meat, and some of the common and cruel industry practices involving animal husbandry and where our "food" comes from. Hearing my own words tumbling out of his mouth made me feel really supported. Don't go telling everybody, but I think I actually might have teared up a bit. I didn't know how much I had been heard and understood until Daniel repeated it. It was a pretty gooey moment for me.

AYINDÉ: You can only avoid talking about "it" for so long, and, trust me, they are gonna want to talk about it. You have to show 'em your passionate side at least once so they know it's there. Use your vegan ammo about food politics. How, yes, you do remember bacon and no, it's not helpful when they wave it under your nose. When all else fails, show 'em the DVD; you know the one. It's war! Kidding. It's playful one-upmanship; just replace guns and bombs with love and sex. If they want to fight about food politics, have the argument, but don't have it to win. Just state your point and let it marinate.

Be proactive and plan ahead

ZOË: Let's talk about the semi-awkwardness of eating in a space you're not comfortable in yet.

Since Dan and I met in college, fancy dinners for two weren't an option. What little money we had was spent on more important things, like textbooks and warm beer. My first several nights at Daniel's, the dinner menu went something like this: first course, spaghetti. Second course, Oreos. This was fun for a sugar-fueled second, but the carb-loading didn't exactly get my juices going, nor did it meet my nutritional needs. I was a bit self-conscious complaining about the culinary options, because coupledom was still new, and I didn't want to seem high maintenance. "Make me a seitan pot-pie! Caramelize those onions! What?! No sesame oil? Get outta me."

Eventually I realized that I could avoid seeming high-maintenance if I planned and packed my own meals. I started showing up with snacks stashed in my purse and would often wander out of

CAN I LOVE SOMEONE WHO EATS ANIMALS?

the bedroom with an apple or a bag of nuts, leaving him to wonder at my resourcefulness...or make a mental note that I was seemingly part of the squirrel family.

Once I got super comfy, I started leaving food in his cabinet and fridge. A little bit of almond milk and some tempeh don't take up too much real estate, and you could bet his roommates weren't going to touch the stuff. If you forget to plan, there is always peanut butter and a spoon...

Proactivity also works with things like vegan contraception. I like to get cruelty-free condoms so I don't have to cringe when my guy whips out his own weapon of choice. I got it covered! Literally...

AYINDÉ: I was not very proactive with Ginger in the beginning. I was lazy, and as I look back, I realize I really didn't put any effort into choosing places at all. When it came to going out to eat, I let her do the work. Why? Well, I didn't eat out a lot because I'm a chef, hello. But Ginger loved going out to eat. It was a big part of her life, and when you merge lifestyles you have to be open to new things. So, we'd go out a lot. As I stated before, I like hole-in-the-wall spots, and she liked something with a few stars. Or at least a star. I would think, "You want to eat here, when they have food I can make better myself?" But I still went, because the responsible, adult thing to do is to help your partner, compromise, and not be a dick. I guess I could have titled this point "don't be a dick."

Include them at mealtime, and beyond

ZOË: A lot of divided couples cook separate meals, which, in my opinion, sucks hard. Talk about disharmony at the dinner table! Don't you want to ooh and ahh over the same amazing dish? Connecting over food has always been such an essential part of my relationships. Get down with me at the table, or get on out.

Dinner table divides aside, consider the extra work of creating two separate meals! In many relationships, there is only one cook in the kitchen. I cooked way more than Daniel, who was a professional dish-master in no time. I never cooked two meals, since twice the meals would be twice the hassle, and I had no time for all of that. Plus, I would be damned if I were to cook anything non-vegan. "I love you, but I will never cook you a steak."

Sometimes, cooking two meals makes logical sense if your eating habits just don't coexist, like when parents feed their picky toddler hot dogs every night. If one of you is a gourmand while the other prefers plain-Jane buttered noodles, it can be hard to share a meal regardless of the food politics. So, in my opinion, cooking separate meals should be a last ditch option. If it's either "cook two meals or eat by yourself," then go for the dual food fix—but your partner better be donning their chef hat along with you!

Food aside, you should also try and include your partner in vegan culture, or any culture you subscribe to. If Daniel could make me sit through a midnight showing of The Avengers, I could take him to a veg food festival, dammit. So include your partner in your restauranteering, your food prep, your cooking. Watch some documentaries with them. Eat good food! Have thought-provoking discussions. Enjoy your differences, because it gives you more to talk about.

AYINDÉ: It sounds crazy when you say "include them." I mean, you're in a relationship, of course they're included. But beware of fatigue. With Ginger, she began to get a little tired of eating vegan at home, and when we ate out, she was tired of not being able to share and have the classic dinner experience. Nobody wants to argue when they are hungry, and it became easy avoid any potential bad vibes by just grabbing meals after work on our own and meeting for drinks or dessert afterward. It was an easy work-around, but be careful—it can also be the beginnings of a wedge.

Choose your battles

ZOË: As your relationship progresses, you will find a nice rhythm for navigating your differences. Maybe it's okay if your partner eats meat when you're not around. Maybe you always eat vegan when you dine out, or you take turns picking restaurants every other time. Find out what works, and more importantly, find out where your comfort zone is. Once you've located it, stand by it, and let the rest go.

Personally, I don't make a fuss about what my partner eats as long as it's not in my living space. If they're happy with what they're eating, then who am I to get all up in their food business? Now, if they tried to bring what they're eating into my kitchen, that's a different story. No meat my fridge, buddy! But that's just me. You need to figure out what's most important to you, and choose those battles. Remember, you chose to be one half of this vegan-fusion couple, so don't nitpick or harass. Save up your energy for the points that truly matter to you. Let them conquer the small things so you can win it big when it counts. Also, whenever possible, let your fork speak. A good meal is a good meal, no arguments needed.

AYINDÉ: Ditto.

Don't judge

ZOË: This is a hard one. When something makes so much sense to you—like, you know, not harming animals—it can be really frustrating when someone you're so crazy about just doesn't get it. But think about how hurt you would be if they judged your lifestyle choices. What if, instead of defending my veganism the way Daniel did, I had overheard him saying "Yeah, she's vegan. Ugh." He would have suffered the rest of our relationship on an oral-sexless existence. If your partner isn't judging you, grant them the same courtesy. You made the decision to date an omnivore, so now you have to suck it up and stand by that decision.

AYINDÉ: I'm a Judgey McJudgerton, I know this. It's in my eyes; I can't hide my feelings. I'd say to Ginger that I was okay with her meat-eating, but then I would sit back and judge my little vegan ass off. One morning, I remember Ginger looked up from a hardboiled egg to see what must have been abject loathing on my face. She said, "Wow, you really don't like eggs, huh?" I didn't even know what my face was doing, but it was one of those moments where I said one thing and meant the exact opposite.

Be compassionate

ZOË: That's what we're all about, right? This goes along with non-judgment, but takes it a step further. As important as it is to not feel judged, it is also important to feel supported. It made me so happy when Daniel would check a menu online to see if I could eat there, or scanned ingredients on labels before offering me some of his snack. And so I tried to shoot it right back at him. I didn't wrinkle my nose when he ordered a beef burger or ate chicken at a barbecue. I did, however, refuse to kiss him post hot dog because those things are potent! Hot dog breath for days. Nasty.

AYINDÉ: There is a Sanskrit mantra, Lokah Samhasta Sukino Bhavantu, which means:

"May all beings be happy and free, and may the thoughts, words, and actions of my own life contribute in some way to that happiness and freedom for all."

This is where I had to practice REAL veganism. We often forget to be compassionate to each other, much like our ethical vegan front-liners. But when you date an omnivore, you are signing up to be a teacher. Even though I said don't try to convert them, and I mean it, when you form a bond with someone and are in close proximity to them on a daily basis, you will learn from them, and also teach them. That's what happens in all relationships. It's natural. Love is our greatest teacher.

The best teachers are compassionate, and attentive, and hot. Remember, it works both ways—we learn from each other, so be strong in your choices. Because of the close proximity and not wanting to be the odd man out in your own home, some will go into a relationship vegan and come out omni.

Stories from the Field

Kristin Lajeunesse, Will Travel for Vegan Food

"It's only when you are comfortable and happy being with yourself that you can be happy and in a healthy relationships with someone else. I know it sounds cliché, but I've learned first-hand that it's true. Because what happens is this: you create a life for yourself that you love by doing things that you love. This might sound *woo-woo-y*, but by doing those things, you energetically attract other people who love those things too. You'll naturally be drawn to and pull in someone who will help you grow, become a better human, and aid in the happiness and love that you've created for yourself. I like to say that I'm not looking for someone who is good for me, but someone who is good with me. And vice versa. I wish to be good with someone, not for them."

Recipes to Impress Your Omni

Let their fork do the convincing...

"*At the very core of relationships that work is respect. I don't expect my partner to think the way I do, act the way I do, or love every cause I take up. I do, however, expect respect. And I expect to be respectful in return. That often means communicating and establishing boundaries early, and often, in a relationship. All of these years later it's my husband who says "I follow an omnivore diet and can eat anything. Let's make something (or go somewhere where) we can both eat.*"*

– JL FIELDS, VEGAN, AUTHOR AND FOUNDER OF JL GOES VEGAN

Hearts of Palm Lobster Rolls

Prep time: 5 minutes | Cook time: 15 minutes | Serves 2

I first started working with hearts of palm for a traditional vegan crab cake recipe. But then I thought, what else could I make in the seafood family? Aha! A lobster roll. I re-imagined this New England summertime favorite with South and Central American palm cabbage, while maintaining traditional flavors and textures. Thanks, globalization!

2 1/2 tablespoons grapeseed or safflower oil

1 (14-ounce) can hearts of palm (not packed with sugar), drained and roughly chopped to the consistency of crab meat

1/4 cup chopped celery

1/4 cup diced red bell pepper

1/2 cup chopped onion

1 teaspoon minced garlic

2 teaspoons Old Bay seasoning

1 teaspoon fresh lemon juice

1/4 cup vegan mayonnaise

2 (6-inch) hoagie rolls

Vegan butter

Lemon wedges, to serve

1. Heat 2 tablespoons of the oil in a large skillet over medium-high heat. Add the hearts of palm and sauté for 8 to 10 minutes, stirring occasionally to prevent sticking. Cook until golden brown on all sides. Set aside to cool. Add the celery and peppers and mix well.

2. Heat 1/2 tablespoon oil in a skillet over medium heat. Add the onion and sauté until translucent, 3 to 4 minutes. Add the garlic and sauté for 1 minute.

3. Remove from the heat and add the onion mixture to the hearts of palm. Mix well. Add the Old Bay seasoning, lemon juice, and mayo.

4. Toast the hoagie rolls until golden brown and butter the insides.

5. Divide the hearts of palm mixture between both rolls. Serve warm with wedges of lemon.

Tortilla Chips with Refried Chipotle-Lemon Pinto Beans

Prep time: 8 minutes | Cook time: 10 minutes | Serves 4 | GF, SF

Okay, I'm gonna be frank—this is your après-amour snack. It's more of a "what you have in the kitchen" meal, which everyone knows is the best kind of midnight munch, when the stores are closed, and you've worked up an appetite. Everyone has a bag (or half-eaten bag) of tortillas, a can of beans, and herbs and spices. Eat up, and get ready for round two!

DIP

1 tablespoon coconut oil

1 tablespoon grapeseed or safflower oil

1/2 cup minced onion

1 dried chipotle chile, stemmed, seeded, and minced

1/2 jalapeño chile, stemmed, seeded, and minced

1 tablespoon minced garlic

1 (15-ounce) can vegan refried pinto beans

1/2 teaspoon ground cumin

1/2 teaspoon salt

1 tablespoon fresh lemon juice

1/2 teaspoon salt (more to taste)

CHIPS

6 (5-inch) corn tortillas, cut into quarters

1/2 cup safflower oil

1 teaspoon salt

1 tablespoon nutritional yeast

1 teaspoon chili powder

1 teaspoon paprika

1 teaspoon chipotle powder

1. Dip: Heat the oils in a medium skillet over medium-high heat until hot. Add the onion and sauté until translucent, approximately 5 minutes.

2. Add the garlic and cook for 1 minute.

3. Add the pinto beans and mix well. Cook for approximately 5 more minutes on medium-low. Add cumin, salt, peppers, and lemon juice. Taste and adjust the seasonings, if needed.

4. Chips: Heat the oil in a medium skillet over medium-high heat until hot. Arrange tortilla wedges in the skillet so that they do not overlap, and cook until browned on both sides. Repeat until all the chips are done.

5. Place chips in a bowl lined with paper towels. Season the chips with salt, nutritional yeast, chili powder, paprika, and chipotle powder. Serve with the dip.

Pro-Tip: For more spicy heat, add the jalapeño seeds to the dip.

Sweet and Savory Blue Cornmeal Cornbread

Prep time: 5 minutes | Cook time: 35 minutes | Serves 4 | SF

One of my Twitter followers said you should always have ingredients for cake in the pantry. Well, growing up in a southern household, we always had ingredients for cornbread. To spice it up a little, I like to use blue cornmeal and veggies. It's a twist on a traditional dish, cooked up in a cast-iron pan. Enjoy!

1 cup all-purpose flour

1 cup blue cornmeal

2/3 cup granulated sugar

3 1/2 teaspoons baking powder

1 teaspoon salt

Egg replacer for 1 egg (page 27)

1 cup water

1/3 cup plus 2 teaspoons grapeseed or
    safflower oil, divided

1 cup unsweetened almond milk

1 cup roughly chopped red onion

2 teaspoons garlic

2 teaspoon chopped fresh rosemary

1 teaspoon chopped fresh sage

1 teaspoon dried basil

1/2 teaspoon red pepper flakes

1. Grease a cast iron skillet or casserole dish with a little oil. Set aside. Preheat the oven to 350°F.

2. In a large bowl, combine the flour, cornmeal, sugar, baking powder, and salt.

3. In a separate bowl, combine the egg mixture with 1/3 cup oil and the almond milk. Mix well.

4. Using a rubber spatula, fold the wet ingredients gently into the dry ingredients.

5. In a medium skillet over medium high heat, heat the remaining 2 teaspoons oil. Add the onion and sauté until it become translucent. Add the garlic, rosemary, sage, basil, and red pepper flakes and sauté for 1 to 2 minutes.

6. Use a rubber spatula to fold the vegetable mixture into the cornmeal mixture. Pour the mixture into the prepared skillet and bake for 35 minutes. Test by pressing a toothpick into the center. If it comes out clean, it's done.

Tuscan Quinoa Pilaf Stuffed Peppers

Prep time: 10 minutes | Cook time: 45 minutes | Serves 2 | GF, SFO

My quinoa pilafs were a favorite. Ginger and I even joked about moving to Austin to start a quinoa business together. Ah, those were the days. Anyway, I was always experimenting with new quinoa recipes. Our weekly Sunday dinners became my test kitchen set. I experimented with a variety of flavors—Mexican, Italian, and more. Eventually, we landed on a favorite staple: Tuscan quinoa. I love the combination of colored bell peppers; the subtle, sweet flavor of red, green, and orange peppers is delicious when stuffed with this nutty, savory quinoa hash. It's light, yet satiating. This recipe can be used as an hors d'oeuvre or an entrée. Use a soy-fee vegan cheese to make this soy-free.

5 cups water, divided

1/2 cup quinoa, well rinsed

1/4 cup grapeseed or safflower oil

1/4 cup chopped onion

1/4 cup chopped red bell pepper

1 teaspoon minced garlic

1 teaspoon chopped fresh rosemary

1 teaspoon chopped fresh sage

1 teaspoon ground fennel seed

2 tablespoon capers, divided

Salt

4 small bell peppers, any color, tops
    sliced off, seeded and cored

1/2 cup shredded vegan mozzarella or
    your fave vegan cheese

1. In a medium saucepan over medium-high heat, bring 1 cup of the water to a boil. Add the quinoa and lower the heat to medium. Cover and cook until the water evaporates, 10 to 15 minutes. Preheat the oven to 350°F.

2. Heat the oil in a large skillet over medium-high heat. Add the onion and sauté until translucent, 3 to 5 minutes. Add the bell pepper, garlic, rosemary, sage, and fennel seed. Sauté for 1 minute.

3. Stir in the cooked quinoa. Mix well and continue to sauté for approximately 5 minutes. Add 1 tablespoon of the capers and salt to taste. Remove from the heat.

4. Bring the remaining 4 cups of water to a boil. Add 1 tablespoon of salt to pot of boiling water. Using tongs, add the peppers to the boiling water and boil for about 5 minutes, until the color of the peppers brightens. Remove with tongs and drain. Cool peppers to room temperature.

5. Using a spoon, stuff the quinoa mixture into the peppers, packing down until filled. Set the peppers in a cupcake pan and cover each of the peppers with shredded cheese. Bake for 15 minutes. Remove from the oven and top with the remaining 1 tablespoon capers. Serve hot.

Hearts of Baltimore Crab Cakes

Prep time: 10 minutes | Cook time: 10 minutes | Serves 2 | GF, SFO

The very first time I went to Baltimore to visit my mom's side of the family, they wanted to take me to Inner Harbor for crab cakes. My mom told them we were vegan, but the family was like "No baby, it's not meat, just crab." Clearly we did not indulge, but they talked so much about these crab cakes, I was interested in learning what the fuss was about. Maryland crab cakes are traditionally oversized, and I wanted to recreate them using hearts of palm and traditional seasonings. I make them gluten-free and pair them with a garlicky dill aïoli. I don't know if it's spot on, but from what I hear, it's pretty darn close. Use a soy-free mayo to make this soy-free.

GARLICKY DILL AÏOLI

1/2 cup vegan mayonnaise

1 tablespoon fresh lemon juice

1 tablespoon chopped fresh dill

1 teaspoon minced garlic

CRAB CAKES

3 tablespoons grapeseed or safflower
    oil, divided, plus more for frying

1 (14-ounce) can hearts of palm, (not
    packed in sugar), roughly chopped
    to the consistency of crab meat

1/4 cup chopped celery

1/4 cup diced red bell pepper

1/2 cup chopped onion

2 teaspoons minced garlic

2 teaspoons Old Bay Seasoning

1 teaspoon cornstarch

1/4 cup vegan mayonnaise

BREADING

1/2 cup gluten-free bread crumbs, or
    more

1 tablespoon Old Bay Seasoning

Lemon wedges, to serve

Pro-Tip: If hearts of palm and vegan mayo are not available in your area, you can find them by searching online under the shopping tab on Google.

1. Garlicky Dill Aïoli: Combine all the ingredients in a small bowl. Mix well and add salt and pepper to taste. Set in the fridge to keep cool.

2. Crab Cakes: Heat 2 tablespoons of the oil in a large skillet over medium-high heat. Add the hearts of palm and sauté for 8 to 10 minutes, stirring occasionally to prevent sticking. Cook until golden brown on all sides. Set aside to cool. Add the celery and peppers and mix well.

3. Heat 1 tablespoon of the oil in a skillet over medium-heat heat. Add the onions and sauté until translucent, 2 to 3 minutes. Add the garlic and sauté for 1 minute.

4. Remove from the heat, add to the hearts of palm, and mix well. Add the Old Bay seasoning, cornstarch, and mayo.

5. Transfer the mixture to a mixing bowl and mix well. Set aside to cool to room temperature, then shape the mixture into four round patties.

6. Breading: In a shallow bowl, combine the bread crumbs and Old Bay seasoning, stirring to mix. Coat the patties with the breadcrumb mixture and refrigerate for 20 minutes.

7. Heat about 3 tablespoons oil in a medium skillet over medium-high heat until hot and shimmering. Carefully place the patties in the skillet and cook until golden brown on each side, approximately 2 minutes per side. Watch closely to prevent burning. Transfer the cooked patties to a plate lined with paper towels to drain any excess oil. Serve hot, topped with the aïoli, with lemon wedges on the side.

Tempeh Fries with Dill Avocado Dip

Prep time: 5 minutes | Cook time: 10 minutes | Serves 2 | GF

I started working with tempeh in my NYC executive chef days and revisited this sprouted soy protein while touring with India.Arie. There are a million different ways to use it, and I found that out because it was the only soy protein India could eat. Once, while I was in the process of making a braised tempeh dish, she ate a piece of plain cooked tempeh which was cooling on a plate. She then continued to eat all of them off the plate, just like that. "Can you make fries?" she asked me? "No, you make fries with potatoes," I responded. But, since the client gets what the client wants, I decided to try it. Next, I needed a dip. India's diet restricted acids and mayo, so it had to be something else creamy and savory. Enter the avocado. When I paired it with dill, I was thinking ranch, and the combination is quite excellent.

1/4 cup grapeseed or safflower oil

1 (8-ounce) package tempeh, cut into French fry sized sticks

Salt and black pepper

2 cloves garlic, chopped

1/4 cup chopped fresh dill

1 cup water

1 ripe avocado, halved, pitted, and peeled

1 tablespoon grapeseed or safflower oil

1 teaspoon lemon juice

1. Heat the oil in a medium skillet over medium-high heat until hot and shimmering. Add the tempeh and cook until golden brown on all sides, turning the tempeh with tongs, 5 to 7 minutes. Season with salt and pepper to taste. Use tongs to remove the tempeh from the skillet and transfer to a paper towel.

2. In a blender, combine the garlic, dill, water, avocado, oil, and lemon juice. Blend until combined. Be careful not to over-blend, as this will change the consistency of the avocado. Season with salt to taste.

3. Transfer the dip to a serving bowl. Serve with the tempeh fries. If not serving right away, press a sheet of plastic wrap snugly on the surface of the dip to limit oxygen exposure and prevent the dip from turning brown.

"At first I wasn't too open to the idea of the person I was dating becoming a vegan. I think it was because I didn't understand it and it just seemed like a hassle to cook separate meals. But when you are in a relationship things change and you have to adapt to keep her happy." — JOEY, OMNIVORE

Braised Tempeh with Carrot Chips

Prep time: 10 minutes | Cook time: 25 minutes | Serves 2 to 4 | GF

While singer India.Arie was in the process of making her album, she would occasionally have dinner parties. As her personal chef, that meant I was cooking. At this point, I was reinventing tempeh in as many ways as possible, so she wouldn't become bored. The flavor, temperature, and texture of this dish are usually found in a more high-end restaurant, with the cool crispness of the carrots contrasting the heat of the tempeh. When approaching this recipe, be sure to follow the instructions closely, paying attention to temperatures to create the max affect. It is a great hors d'oeuvre.

1/4 cup safflower oil

4 ounces tempeh, cut crosswise into 1/8-inch slices

1/2 cup diced onion

3 cloves garlic, minced

1 teaspoon dried sage

1/2 teaspoon red pepper flakes

1/2 teaspoon dried basil

1/2 teaspoon dried thyme

1/4 cup low-sodium wheat-free tamari

1/4 cup water

2 large carrots, peeled

2 tablespoons chopped scallion, for garnish

1. Heat the oil in a medium skillet over medium-high heat until hot and shimmering. Add the tempeh and cook until golden brown on all sides, 5 to 7 minutes. With tongs, remove the tempeh from the skillet and set aside on a paper-towel-lined plate.

2. In the same skillet, add the onion and sauté until translucent, 2 to 3 minutes.

3. Add the garlic, sage, red pepper flakes, basil, and thyme. Stir in the tamari and water and add the tempeh back into the skillet. Cover and braise on low heat for 10 to 15 minutes.

4. Cut the carrots on the diagonal, about 1/8-inch thick, roughly the same length as the tempeh. You should have approximately 12 slices. Place the carrot slices in the refrigerator and keep cold until ready to serve.

5. To serve, arrange the chilled carrots on plate, place a piece of hot tempeh on top of each carrot slice, and garnish with chopped green onion. Serve as an appetizer or main meal.

Devil's Pot Pie

Prep time: 15 minutes | Cook time: 45 minutes | Makes 8 slices

When brainstorming holiday main dishes, I asked my Facebook friends what holiday food they missed most, and I heard a resounding "OMG I miss pot pie." You had me at pie; say no more. I took on this savory American classic. This is gravy, veggies, and a fluffy crust all in one magical pie. Why devil's pie? Well, the wordplay on seitan has become a tradition in just about every menu I make. It's a signature, kinda like Carol Burnett's ear-tug thing. (This means nothing if you're under 30.)

1 double pie crust (double quiche crust recipe, page 36)

3 tablespoons vegan butter

1 tablespoon refined coconut oil

1 cup chopped leeks, white and light green parts only

1/2 cup chopped celery

1 cup chopped carrots

1 teaspoon minced garlic

1 teaspoon minced habanero chiles, stemmed, seeded, and minced

1 tablespoon minced fresh sage

2 teaspoons dried basil

2 teaspoon chopped fresh thyme

1/3 cup all-purpose flour

1 3/4 cups vegetable broth

1 tablespoon low-sodium wheat-free tamari

1/2 cup unsweetened soy milk

2 cups asparagus, woody ends removed, cut into 1/2-inch pieces

1 cup frozen peas

1 1/2 cups diced seitan (see Note)

1. Make the pie crust as directed. Arrange the bottom pie crust in a pie plate and set it in the freezer. Preheat the oven to 375°F.

2. In a medium saucepan over medium-high heat, melt the vegan butter and coconut oil. Add the leeks, celery, carrots, garlic, habaneros, sage, basil, and thyme. Sauté until the vegetables are tender, 5 to 7 minutes. Whisk in the flour, mixing constantly. This should brown into a light roux. Add the broth, tamari, and soy milk, whisking until thickened. Fold in the asparagus, peas and seitan. Cook for an additional 5 minutes on low simmer.

3. Add the mixture to the pie shell and top with your second pie shell, crimping the edge to seal. Brush the top crust with a little oil. Poke a few holes in the top to vent the steam. Bake for 35 to 40 minutes. You can tell when it's done when it's a golden brown color and smells like pot pie! Remove from the oven and allow to sit for several minutes before serving.

Note: You can use storebought seitan if you like, but if you want to make your own, make a half batch of the seitan recipe on page 120.

Pro-Tip: Use gloves when cutting the habañero chile, and wash your cutting board with soap and warm water afterward.

Stories from the Field

Elizabeth Castoria, author of *How to Be Vegan*

"Before I started seeing my current guy, I had only seriously dated vegans for the last ten-ish years. I honestly thought that I couldn't be in a relationship with someone who didn't think about animals in the same way I do, that it would be too surreal and sad to watch someone eat animals routinely. With previous dudes, having veganism in common was a huge part of my identity within the relationship. But when Ricky came along, we started seeing each other without having any intention of getting into a relationship. About a year later, we realized that we were in love. We'd already built a solid relationship, in which we accepted each other and didn't have any expectations for the other person, so it wasn't weird to me that he ate meat.

The best tip I can give is just to really be honest with yourself—which is pretty important in all aspects of relationships. Also, be with someone who enhances your life."

*"You lucky f*cks."*

Even for those in vegan-on-vegan lalaland, it's going to take so much more than a shared interest in animal welfare and killer veggie-braising skills to make a relationship work.

You may be wondering why you should take tips on meeting and dating vegans from two people who have never dated another vegan. Well, you have a good point there. Our answer is simple: an abundance of research.

We've been trolling, er, polling, our online network for several years doing research for this exact book. We've made our coupled-up vegan friends uncomfortable by prying into their love lives—and even sex lives. Any chance to be nosy under the guise of empirical research...

And it's not as if we haven't tried to date vegans (more on that in a moment), so throw us a non-literal bone here. Also, if you're reading this book, you're probably struggling with the whole vegan-on-vegan thing yourself. Just sayin'.

AYINDÉ: You can see that there are many different varieties of vegans, so even if you do meet one, it still may be hard to match up. You may not see eye-to-eye on your $800 shoes, or his "vintage leather." Or worse, you meet the perfect vegan—I mean, your real dream girl or guy—and then you end up in the friend zone. Ouch is right. True story. Here is an excerpt from a real conversation I had with my dream vegan mate, the one who got (very far) away:

Me: Hi, how have you been?
Her: Oh, I've been fantastic.
Me: Good to hear. Hey, I was wondering if you wanted to get together and maybe grab a bite, like a date?
Her: Oh, Ayindé, how sweet. But I just don't think of you that way.
Me: But what about all that flirting?
Her: No, no, Ayindé. I was not flirting with you, I'm just European. I value our friendship too much to ever flirt with you. Can you hold a second?... Ayindé? Can I call you right back? I'm so sorry. Ciao.

Okay, first off, she was West African. I was home-schooled, but I'm pretty sure that ain't in Europe. Still waiting on that call, by the way.

In the end, you may end up with a great friend to swap ancient grain recipes with while you try to figure out why she won't dump the omni-anderthal and see how great your vegan kids would be.

I mean, with our veganism combined, we could have been the ultimate power couple, better than Brangelina, the Smiths, and even the Obamas! Anyway. If you meet your dream vegan mate and they hand you a hearty helping of rejection, then maybe go with the pescetarian and hope to convert 'em…. *slapping wrist* *Bad vegan!* Accept everyone for who they are, blah, blah, blah. I know, I know.

Or maybe you're in a vegan-on-vegan setup because your once-omni mate decided to go vegan! You were just effing about, and all of a sudden they announced their supreme candidacy for your requirements for a mate. Thanks, universe. They are three weeks into their new vegan thing, and it's all you can do to stay cool. Resist the urge to help too much. I mean, let them know if they need help, you're available, but let them get their footing on their new path. And let them know that just because they're vegan now, it changes nothing as far as commitment goes! Unless you're ready to take it there. You know. Mm…MM… I can't say it…

ZOË: Marriage.

AYINDÉ: Thanks, homie. After you find what you claim to want, and if you think your relationship is ready, then go forward and make vegan babies with someone as crazy as you. From what I've heard, parenthood is a whole different game.

ZOË: The closest I have ever come to dating an herbivore is the time I went on a date with a vegetarian. Actually, we went on two dates, but it was the first that was so memorable. I used to call it the "worst" date, but I need to clarify that the person I was with was very lovely—the evening was only bad due to circumstance; the date ended with me sopping wet, and not in the fun way.

Here we go.

For the sake of anonymity, I am re-naming my date Carl, after Carl Perkins, due to his affinity for suede shoes—this will come into play soon. Our first date technically was not our first date, because Carl was someone I had known from summer camp back in the days of my moody, hormonal youth. By "someone I had known," I mean we spent many hours nibbling earlobes in the woods. However, I think those dates—those are dates when you're thirteen—expire after a decade, so I will call this specific warm summer evening our first date.

You can imagine my excitement. I was freshly single, and someone I had a huge crush on when I was younger wanted to take me out. I remembered thirteen-year-old Carl as this super cool guitar-playing punk rocker with blue spiked hair, which made him a total babe in 2002. Since reconnecting, Carl had grown up—kind, vegetarian, interesting, vegetarian, handsome, vegetarian, employed, and a vegetarian. Basically, things had never looked better. And, did I mention, vegetarian?

Carl and I made plans to grab dinner before I rendezvoused with some friends for the evening. (It's always good to have an out on a first date.) We were in New York, and when I got to the train station to meet him, he announced several things. The first was that he wanted to eat at one of New York's best vegan restaurants, Blossom, which sounded great to me. The second was that it was going to rain, and that he brought a spare pair of shoes. A what? Glancing down at his shoes, which were a very nice looking pair of oxfords, I wondered why he didn't just wear shoes that were down with H_2O? I guess even guys think about first-date footwear.

So, Carl was all good with two pairs of shoes. I, on the other hand, was not dressed for the rain. My shirt was white. My skirt was way too tiny for hopping in and out of puddles. I had been too excited about the date to check the weather, but I was not worried. I was going on a date with a handsome guy who didn't eat animals, and so what if he was kind of high-maintenance about his shoes, right? Right.

We started walking toward Blossom. When it started to sprinkle slightly, Carl pulled out an umbrella. He had by then stopped under some scaffolding to change his shoes.

So we walked. Carl held his umbrella, and in the other hand, a bag with his suede shoes. Unfortunately, the bag wasn't water-proof—a hole in your planning, Carl! So, naturally he held the bag of shoes under the umbrella. And where was I? In the rain. I think he was at least sort of trying to get all four of us under the umbrella (me, him, and both his shoes...), but it wasn't really happening.

Blossom was a forty-minute walk away, and I was getting progressively more wet. My skirt was riding up and sticking to me, making me look progressively sluttier with every block we covered.

We got to Blossom. It was super fancy in there, and I looked like a skanky sewer rat, but it was cool because we aren't allowed in anyway—we needed a reservation, which we didn't have.

We ended up going to three different places before finding somewhere to seat us—everywhere was packed since no one wanted to be wandering in the rain. Once we were seated at this little vegan Chinese place with a bistro-y feel, I ran to the bathroom and sat under the hand dryer for 10 minutes, because at that point you could wring a glass of ice cold water out of my undies.

Despite the circumstances, I was still pretty stoked to be out with Carl. I was just back in the dating game, and Carl was both new and familiar at the same time; remember the rampant ear nibbling, which was a thing then. Carl was really nice the whole date, and we had fun despite the wetness. In retrospect, I have no clue why we didn't grab a cab. Cab grabbing is usually easy when your skirt is plastered to your thighs.

We even went on a second date. It didn't rain, we made reservations at Blossom, and then we went to the park where he taught me how to play chess. Freakin' adorable, right? I was basically the lead in an indie film with Owen Wilson. Or Luke Wilson? I don't know, one of the Wilson brothers.

On paper, Carl was a total catch. However, no matter how hard I tried, I couldn't get over the shoe thing. Not because they were suede or anything, but because he brought an extra pair of footwear on a date that didn't require an extra pair of footwear. Had we, say, been rock climbing or hiking, it would have made more sense. It seemed so incredibly high maintenance in a way that was a red flag for me. I need an easygoing guy, because, well, I tend to over-think everything, and there needs to be a balance.

There were other things, too. I'm not one to let one shoe fail ruin a relationship. We just weren't compatible, and I really, really, really wanted to be, because single, attractive, smart, compassionate men who don't have a drug addiction or an alarming attachment to their mother seem to be

scarce these days. And then, of course, there was the fact that he was holding his shoes under his umbrella the whole time. Basically, men, take note here: if you're out with a lady and it starts to rain, your shoes should never ever end up dryer than your date.

Okay, vegansexuals. Let's say you find a veg-friendly love interest. Maybe you met online or through a friend or at a local meet-up. You make plans to go on a date, and you're so damned excited, because finding a suitable vegan partner is hard! Unfortunately, once you're out on your date, instead of fireworks, your chemistry is stalling like a dead car battery. Here is how to survive a zombie date:

1. With a whole lot of humor. By the time Carl and I were turned away from our second restaurant, I had adoringly told Carl this was the worst date I had ever been on, and that I would most likely be writing about it in the near future. Also I made fun of his attachment to his shoes at every possible chance—I mean, you go on a date with a VEGAN and babysit your suede shoes the whole night? Just sayin'.

2. With a positive attitude—I know a lot of girls who would have been pretty cranky by the time they found a place to eat. But I don't think I ever stopped smiling, because then I would have been cold AND wet AND miserable.

3. With compassion. Okay, I kind of failed on this one, because I wrote about the whole thing on the Internet. I had just started the original Lusty Vegan column over on iEatGrass, and I was supposed to be chronicling my newly single vegan life, like Sex in the City but without the nice apartment, and a closet full of kitchen equipment, not shoes. Carl read the post (titled "How to Survive the Worst Date Ever") and texted me later, understandably annoyed about it. Sorry again, Carl!

However, just because you didn't make a connection doesn't mean you have to totally write off your date. Since single, eligible vegans are hard to come by, pay it forward and set them up with a friend or at least try and salvage the romantic flop into your own friendship. (In the end, Carl didn't want to be my friend. Probably because of the Internet thing. And probably because I am writing about it again here. I guess those moments of youthful woodland ear nibbling meant nothing to him, after all.)

For single vegans

So you're looking to meet a vegan, eh? One who is not going to alienate your family members at Thanksgiving with tales from the slaughterhouse. One who is a total kitchen wizard and knows that vegan cooking has evolved way past steaming raw veggies or molding nuts into a loaf. Seriously, you want a compassionate foodie that can flambé and sauté like a boss. Okay, maybe you will just settle for a big heart and winning smile and moderate microwaving skills.

If you're a man looking for a vegan lady, you've got an easier road ahead of you, as there are more vegan girls out there. But even single vegan dudesters have been writing in to iEatGrass, inquiring how to meet a vegan lady—even ones in booming veg-friendly metropolises like Los Angeles!

So maybe you're all prepped. You have a bedside table stocked with Sir Richard's condoms and cruelty-free toys, yet you can't find a plant-based playmate to share a magical evening with.

SPREAD THE WORD.

IF YOU ARE REALLY SET ON FINDING A VEGAN PARTNER,

TELL EVERYONE YOU KNOW.

What's a lusty vegan to do? Here are a few tips on finding a vegan bed buddy, be it for a night of excitement or a lifetime of spooning and vegan baby-making.

1. Stalk your local hot spots. If you're still in the bar-hopping time of your life, then the obvious choice for meeting a mate is at a bar. But considering that bars are not the normal vegan hang-out, and you probably aren't looking for an average man or woman (because vegans are sooo above average, hello!) a bar probably is not your best shot. Unless, of course, it's a vegan bar! Those do exist in Brooklyn, and Portland, and probably Austin. Anyway, what you need to do is head to a vegan-friendly hangout. This can differ depending on your location. A yoga studio with a raw juice bar probably attracts a heavy cruciferous crowd. A vegan-friendly coffee shop is also a good bet. Set up your computer or bring a good book and eye-stalk everyone that walks in the door. See something you like? Strike up a convo. Another tip? When you head to that vegan spot, wear that lucky "I Heart Kale" shirt, or even better, an "I Eat Grass" tee. That way, you're easy to spot, and obviously very hip.

2. Spread the word. If you are really set on finding a vegan partner, tell everyone you know. I mean, everyone. You never know who has a cute, single, vegan co-worker or gym buddy. This is how my mother met her life partner. She started telling everyone she was on the lookout, and one of her friends happened to know a single, crunchy, outdoorsy dude from yoga. Ten years and two farms later, the pair is still adorably inseparable. If no one knows you're looking, they can't set you up. However, be specific in what you're looking for. If you're just looking for a one-night stand or short fling, it may be best not to date

friends of friends, as things can quickly become more awkward than the time my doula aunt cornered Daniel at a family party and started telling him what an amazing organ the vagina is.

3. Get involved. I know I am telling you to look look look for a vegan mate, but often you find someone when you're not looking. Get involved with things in your community you're passionate about, and you are more likely to find someone with similar interests. When you have the same routine (yoga, work, drinks in the same social circle) week after week, it's hard to meet fresh faces. So volunteer at a shelter, local community garden, or vegan organization. Even if you don't meet someone date-able there, you may make new friends (who could possibly set you up!) or at least get involved in a passion project and give back. Good karma points for you!

4. Get online. Online dating isn't for everyone, but there are a good amount of online sources for vegans these days. There are also vegan speed dating events. You don't have to join a network specifically for singles; any vegan meet-up will do.

5. Hit the grocery store. If you want to find a vegan mate, hang out in the healthy person section of your grocery store and start eye-ballin' carts. See a cutie with a cruelty-free load? Follow them around in a non-creepy way for a bit, check their fingers for wedding rings, and then sidle up to them in the non-dairy section and start a friendly commentary on their selection, "Hm, I've never tried that cashew-coconut milk blend—is it any good?"

For coupled vegans

So you've found a vegan mate, huh? Lucky you. Whether you're a strict vegansexual or just happened to find a connection at a plant-based potluck, you may be thinking you're set. Not so fast, you little lettuce muncher!

There are several different varieties of vegans (refer to our intro for a rundown), and some of us follow our own rules about what it means to be cruelty-free. Some don't agree with keeping pets, while others have rescued so many dogs, they basically have an entire animal shelter going on in their house. Some vegans wear recycled (i.e. used) leather. Some eat honey. No two vegans are the same, and while dating a vegan makes it more likely the two of you will connect, veganism is not a magical compatibility blanket! Before you commence with the vegan baby-making, be sure veganism isn't the only appealing thing about your partner.

Stories from the Field

Joshua Katcher, founder of TheDiscerningBrute.com and Brave GentleMan

"My veganism has always played into my dating and relationships. My current relationship, which is going on four years, is with someone who was already vegan when we met. He was introduced to me through a friend. After having gone on some disastrous first-dates and a couple of depressing short-term flings with people who had a lot of misconceptions about veganism, it was a relief to be able to talk about things aside from why I'm vegan or respond to the same twenty questions followed by accusations of being defensive and judgmental. (Who's the defensive one?) In the past, when I dated people for longer than a few weeks, the issue of veganism would inevitably surface. The danger of the teacher/student dynamic can neutralize chemistry in the case that your partner wants to explore it, or on the other hand, an unwillingness to consider animal ethics can be a source of alienation and resentment. Being in a relationship with another ethical vegan feels great because you know you share some very specific principles and values. It also makes sex better. There's an unspoken knowledge that has profound implications about our worldview, our values, and how we live. And I'd go further and say it's not about "beliefs" per se, but a shared pursuit of truth that is a perpetual journey."

The Grassmuncher's Menu

Soups, salads, and sandwiches

Tempeh Piccata Hoagie	92
French Lentil Soup	94
Coconut Rosemary Soup	95
Braised Tempeh Salad with Chimichurri Dressing	96
Granny's Waldorf Salad	98
Pickled Fennel Salad	99
Roasted Corn and Potato Chowder	100
Sriracha Tempeh Sliders	102

"I met my current vegan partner on Instagram! No joke. I posted a food pic from my favorite restaurant, and he posted one from the same place that very day. We started following each other and commenting on each other's pics, and eventually he asked for my email and asked me out. Big win for social media!"

– TINA, VEGAN

Tempeh Piccata Hoagie

Prep time: 8 minutes (plus time to marinate tempeh) | Cook time: 10 minutes | Serves 2 to 3

For this recipe, I drew inspiration from Italy. Actually, I drew inspiration from Ginger, who made tempeh piccata for me on a date night. I adapted the recipe and used it for my teaching classes in NYC. At one point, a gentleman asked if I could make it as a sandwich, and everything came together—the savory marinade paired with the tangy mayo and juicy tempeh, all wrapped up in a handheld meal.

AÏOLI

1/2 cup vegan mayonnaise

2 tablespoons fresh lemon juice

2 tablespoons chopped fresh parsley

1 tablespoon capers

TEMPEH

3 cloves garlic, pressed

2 tablespoons dried basil

2 tablespoons dried oregano

2 tablespoons chili powder

2 teaspoons minced fresh thyme

2 teaspoons rubbed sage

1/2 cup low-sodium wheat-free tamari

1/4 cup fresh lemon juice

1/4 cup water

Salt

1 (8-ounce) package tempeh, sliced
    into 3 cutlets

1/2 cup unsweetened soy milk

1/2 cup all-purpose flour

1/2 cup safflower oil

2 (6-inch) hoagie rolls

TOPPINGS

Grilled onions

Lettuce leaves

Tomato slices

1. Aïoli: Combine all the aïoli ingredients in a small bowl. Mix well. Set aside or cover and refrigerate until needed

2. Tempeh: In a small bowl, combine the garlic, basil, oregano, chili powder, thyme, sage, tamari, lemon juice, water, and salt to taste. Add the tempeh cutlets and marinate for 30 to 45 minutes. For a stronger flavor, marinate for up to 60 minutes.

3. Place the soy milk in a shallow bowl. Place the flour in a separate shallow bowl. Remove the tempeh from the marinade, dredge (or dip) the tempeh in the milk, then coat it with flour and shake off any excess. Set the tempeh aside.

4. Heat the oil in a large skillet over medium high heat until hot and shimmering. Add the tempeh and, using tongs, flip and cook on each side for approximately 3 minutes, or until golden brown. Use tongs to remove the tempeh and transfer it to a plate lined with a paper towel. Repeat until all the tempeh is cooked.

5. Toast the hoagie rolls under the broiler until they reach the desired crispness. Spread the reserved aïoli on both sides of the bread. Add the reserved tempeh and top with grilled onions, lettuce, and tomato. Serve hot.

French Lentil Soup

Prep time: 5 minutes | Cook time: 30 minutes | Serves 4 | GF, SFO

Lentil soup is easily the most underrated soup around. Lentils have a natural nutty flavor that create an earthy and full-flavored broth, they're super filling, and they offer a great source of protein. During my New York life, there was a small café up the street from my acting school in Manhattan, and the only vegan thing they had on their menu was the lentil soup. Twice a week, in between classes, I'd get the lentil soup and doctor it up with some salt and pepper (and a little hot sauce, of course). My own recipe needs nothing more than a spoon and good piece of bread. This is also a great recipe to cook and eat from all week. Use a soy-free cream (or omit it) to make this soy-free.

1 cup dry French lentils

4 cups water

1/4 cup chopped celery

1/4 cup chopped onion

1 tablespoon chopped fresh thyme

1 teaspoon minced garlic

1 teaspoon chopped fresh sage

1/2 cup chopped carrots

2 tablespoons olive oil

1 tablespoon black truffle oil, optional

Salt and black pepper

Vegan sour cream, optional

1. Combine the lentils and water in a medium saucepan and bring to a boil. Once the water has begun to boil, add the celery, onion, thyme, garlic, and sage. Reduce the heat to medium-low. Cover and cook for approximately 20 minutes.

2. Add the carrots and cook for approximately 10 minutes or until desired tenderness. Finish with olive oil, black truffle oil, if using, and salt and pepper, to taste. Top with vegan sour cream, if using.

"I live in a city where vegan food is hard to come by, and I used to bring my foodie girlfriend vegan snacks instead of flowers... She would be so thrilled, and it was the easiest romantic gesture ever." – JASON, OMNIVORE

Coconut Rosemary Soup

Prep time: 7 minutes | Cook time: 10 minutes | Serves 4 | GF, SF

It was 2013. I was on tour with India.Arie, stuck in the middle of America, and she asked for "something different." I hate that request, but then again, I love it because of the challenge it gives me. It was cold outside and I had a can of coconut milk and some veggies and herbs, so I got to work. The result turned out well; the subtle sweetness of coconut paired with the pungent flavor of rosemary offers a natural warming property. I like to serve it over quinoa or brown rice.

1 tablespoon grapeseed or safflower oil

1/4 cup chopped onion

2 tablespoons minced garlic

1/2 cup chopped carrots

1/4 cup chopped celery

1 cup chopped button mushrooms

1/4 cup chopped green onions

1 cup chopped cauliflower

1/2 cup cut green beans

1/4 cup canned, fresh, or frozen corn kernels

2 tablespoons chopped rosemary

1 (13-ounce) can unsweetened coconut milk

Salt and black pepper

1. Heat the oil in a large saucepan over medium-high heat. Add the onion and sauté until translucent, 2 to 3 minutes.

2. Add the garlic, carrots, celery, mushrooms, green onions, cauliflower, green beans, and corn and cook for about 10 minutes.

3. Stir in the rosemary and coconut milk and simmer on low heat until the vegetables are tender. Season with salt and pepper to taste.

Braised Tempeh Salad with Chimichurri Dressing

Prep time: 5 minutes | Cook time: 25 minutes | Serves 2 | GF

The year was 2009, and it was a cold winter in NYC. I was just getting into my groove in Union Square as an executive chef at Jivamuktea Café. At the cafe, we had a full salad menu, but one salad in particular stood out—so much so that it caught the attention of Mr. Russell Simmons. After he tweeted rave reviews about it, I received a call from the New York Times looking for a quote for an article and suddenly I was on the map in NYC. The sauce was originally a Thai peanut sauce, but I always made a chef's special with the tangy chimichurri sauce. Soon word got out that the chef preferred this sauce and people would ask for the "one the chef gets." This lil recipe did so much for me, how could I not include it in this book?

1 recipe braised tempeh (page 79)

DRESSING

1/3 cup lemon juice

1/2 cup olive oil

1/4 cup chopped fresh cilantro

1/4 cup chopped onion

2 tablespoons minced garlic

1 tablespoon smoked paprika

2 teaspoons dried oregano

1/4 teaspoon cayenne pepper

1 teaspoon coarse sea salt

SALAD

1 (5-ounce) package mixed greens

1 cup chopped English cucumber

1/4 cup thinly sliced red onion

1/2 cup cherry tomatoes, sliced

1. Tempeh: Using the recipe from page 79, cut the tempeh into 1/8-inch thick slices. Following the tempeh braising instructions, cook until brown on both sides. Set aside.

2. Dressing: Combine all the ingredients in a blender and blend until smooth. Add more cayenne or salt to taste. The dressing should be a golden-reddish color. Set aside.

3. Salad: In a large bowl, combine the salad ingredients with the reserved braised tempeh. Add 1/4 cup of the dressing and toss to combine. Serve the remaining dressing on the side. Refrigerate any leftover dressing in a tightly sealed container in the refrigerator.

Granny's Waldorf Salad

Prep time: 5 minutes | Serves 2 to 4 | GF, SFO

I was in a salad-making frenzy a couple of summers ago. Feeling nostalgic, I remembered my maternal grandmother was known her Waldorf salad. I had never had a Waldorf salad before, so I called up my mom and asked why my grandmother liked that salad so much. My mom told me she really enjoyed the combination of flavors and textures. I researched the original, played with it, and added a twist with Rainier cherries, because at the time they were in season. I think I was right with that addition, but I will let you be the judge. Use a soy-free vegan mayo to make this soy-free.

3 tablespoons vegan mayonnaise

1 tablespoon fresh lemon juice

1/2 teaspoon sea salt

1/4 teaspoon white pepper

1 sweet apple, cored and chopped

1/2 cup thinly sliced celery

1/4 cup pitted and sliced Rainier cherries (fresh or frozen)

1/4 cup golden California raisins

1/2 cup lightly toasted walnuts, chopped

2 heads Boston lettuce, washed, dried, and torn

1 teaspoon lemon zest

1. In a medium sized bowl, whisk together the mayonnaise, lemon juice, salt, and white pepper. Mix in the apple, celery, cherries, raisins, and walnuts.

2. Serve on a bed of fresh lettuce and garnish with lemon zest.

WHY WALDORF?

Granny isn't the only one who loves the combo of creamy mayo and crunchy celery. The salad is much older than Granny herself; it came about in the 1890s at the original Waldorf Hotel in New York City. The hotel's maître d', Oscar Tschirky, created the dish, and in 1896 the recipe first appeared in his cookbook, simply titled The Cook Book. Thanks, Oscar!

Pickled Fennel Salad

Prep Time: 30 minutes | Serves 2 to 4 | GF, SF

Fennel grew wild in my old neighborhood of Tacoma, Washington. Fast forward to present day. I was re going through a pickling phase when I came up with this salad. It has both sour and salty notes that marry well with the fibrous sweetness of fennel. Enjoy its acidity on its own or as an addition to your favorite entrée.

1 large fennel bulb, julienned, fronds reserved and coarsely chopped (approximately 2 cups)

1/2 teaspoon sea salt

Juice of 1 lemon

1. Place the chopped fennel in a small bowl and sprinkle it with the salt. Mix well.

2. Add the lemon juice and refrigerate for 30 minutes. Serve by itself or accompanying your favorite dish. You can use the fronds as a garnish and/or save them for making a stock.

5 THINGS YOU DIDN'T KNOW ABOUT FENNEL

1. Fennel has long been thought to boost the female libido, as it contains an estrogen-like substance called estragole. The ancient Egyptians prescribed fennel to increase desire among women, and in the 1930s, it was briefly considered as a source of synthetic estrogen.

2. Fennel is packed with fiber, potassium, and vitamin C.

3. Taste familiar? Fennel's aromatic flavor is extremely similar to licorice and anise, and is often mistaken for one of the two.

4. Fennel contains a volatile oil called anethole that has been shown to reduce inflammation and possibly even help prevent cancer.

5. In Greek mythology, fennel is closely associated with Dionysus, the god of food and wine. The Greeks also believed that it was a fennel stalk that passed down knowledge from the gods to men. Pretty powerful plant.

Roasted Corn and Potato Chowder

Prep time: 8 minutes | Cook time: 30 minutes | Serves 4 | GF, SF

Ah, another recipe from my time as a chef in downtown Manhattan. Soups were big with clients, so my sous chef and I worked to create 25 different soups to rotate daily. They do say that the mark of a good chef is how well they can prepare a soup. This simple soup pairs subtle spicing with creamy potato to create a thick, hearty bowl that soothes and fills. It became a favorite of clients, and a favorite of mine as well. It works best with red potatoes because they still hold their shape after being boiled. You should have chunks of potato to add to the heartiness of the soup itself.

1 pound red potatoes, cut into chunks

2 ribs celery, rough chopped

1/2 medium yellow onion, cut into wedges

3 cups water

2 cups corn kernels

1/4 cup grapeseed or safflower oil

1/3 cup diced red onion

1/2 cup chopped red bell pepper

1/2 cup chopped green bell pepper

2 tablespoons chopped rosemary

1 teaspoon dried basil

1/2 teaspoon red pepper flakes

2 teaspoons salt

1. In a medium soup pot, combine the potatoes, celery, and onion wedges. Cover with the water and bring to a boil, then reduce the heat to medium low. Cover and cook until the potatoes are fork tender, approximately 20 minutes. Preheat the oven to 350°F.

2. Spread the corn kernels on a rimmed baking sheet and drizzle with 2 tablespoons of the oil. Roast the corn until it becomes golden brown, about 25 minutes.

3. Heat the remaining 2 tablespoons of oil in a small skillet over medium-high heat. Add the red onion and bell peppers and sauté until softened, 3 to 5 minutes. Add the rosemary, basil, and red pepper flakes and sauté for 2 to 3 minutes. Remove from the heat.

4. Using a slotted spoon, transfer about half of the potatoes, celery, and onion to a blender. Blend until adding water to get to desired consistency.

5. Pour the mixture back into the soup pot, fold in the reserved sautéed vegetables and corn kernels. Salt to taste. Serve hot.

Sriracha Tempeh Sliders

Prep time: 8 minutes | Cook time: 20 minutes | Serves 4 to 6

By the time I began writing this book, tempeh had become one of my favorite proteins to work with. I've found it makes the best little sliders. These are great are because you get about 4 per standard package of tempeh. Since living in LA, these lil' guys have become a staple in my catering arsenal. Here is a hint; you can replace the sriracha with BBQ sauce if it's too hot for you!

Note: You can find slider buns at Trader Joe's or well-stocked supermarkets. If unavailable, cut hoagie rolls into slider-sized sections.

1/4 cup grapeseed or safflower oil

8 ounces tempeh, cut into 4 squares

1/4 cup chopped onion

2 teaspoons chopped fresh sage

1 teaspoon chopped garlic

1 teaspoon dried basil

1 teaspoon salt

1 1/2 tablespoons sriracha sauce

1 1/2 cups water

8 slider buns, split

Ranch Dressing (page 209)

1/2 red onion, sliced (optional)

1/2 cucumber, sliced (optional)

1. Heat the oil in a medium skillet over medium heat until hot and shimmering. Add the tempeh and cook until browned on both sides, about 4 minutes per side. Repeat until all of the tempeh is cooked.

2. Remove the tempeh to a plate lined with paper towels. Remove half of the oil from the skillet and return the skillet to the heat. Add the onion and sauté for approximately 2 minutes, then add the sage, garlic, basil, and salt and sauté for 1 minute.

3. In a bowl, combine the water and sriracha, stirring to mix. Pour the sriracha water into the skillet and add the tempeh back into skillet. Cover and simmer on low for 10 minutes.

4. Lightly toast the slider buns and arrange a tempeh patty on the bottom half of each bun. Top with the dressing and sliced onion and or cucumber, if using. Serve hot.

"Our shared connection makes everyday things more fun and easy—like exploring neighborhoods and new cities together. But veganism is also a sign of basic things like self-awareness, discipline, a proactive personality, and compassion that I find super sexy and a requirement in a partner."—LEANNE MAI-LY HILGART, FOUNDER OF VAUTE COUTURE

"Can't you just pick around the chicken?"

So your omni partner is down with your vegan lifestyle. Terrific! But their parents—heck, your parents—now, that's another story. Meeting someone else's family is stressful enough, and when you throw veganism into the mix, it's the perfect recipe for a deliciously awkward time. You want this future fam-in-law to like you, really really like you, but you're not about to change your views to get there.

Below are a few stories and tips about enjoying your Sig-O's family without starving all weekend or getting into a fist fight with Uncle Jim Bob the hunting fanatic.

ZOË: I'll begin with the story about "meatless balls." I will never forget the first time I met Daniel's family. It was our junior year in college, and I had driven seven hours to Daniel's parent's house over summer break. As I turned onto his street, I was so nervous about meeting his folks that I thought I might pee my pants. That also may just have been because I hadn't used a restroom in 300 miles or so, but I was too nervous to be sure.

Why so nervous? On top of just meeting his family, I was about to make my mark as The First Girl Danny Brought Home. Despite (or because of) his southern gentlemanliness, Dan had made it all the way to college without a serious girlfriend, which made me feel better about having to follow him into a bathroom just to get his attention. Our relationship probably wouldn't have happened otherwise. So yeah, I was terrified of meeting the family, and my veganism made seven straight days of living (and eating) with the family even more daunting. Talk about colossal pressure.

Daniel's mom was rumored to be an excellent cook, but also a huge Paula Deen fan. She was famous for her holiday cheese balls and some sort of caramel cake that calls for three (!!!) whole sticks of butter. What was I going to eat for the next seven days? And how many times would I have to say "No, eggs aren't vegan either." Aside from my clothes, my bag was stuffed full of the essentials: cruelty-free condoms and nuts.

When I arrived at Daniel's, I called him, too nervous to ring the bell. I was also nervous because there was a carriage parked outside his address, fully outfitted with two horses switching their tails and stomping their hooves as horses do. What was I about to get into?

Daniel came outside to meet me, grabbed my bags, and explained that the horses belonged to a Mennonite family that lived down the block. Welcome to the south, y'all! Before we went inside, we fondled each other up against my

beat up Honda Civic with the type of fervor reserved for those reuniting after a long absence. I felt like I had just returned from war.

After momentarily molesting him through his gym shorts, I froze. What if his parents were watching!? His mom! I put the brakes on our tryst and tried to rub the wrinkles out of my shirt before following Daniel toward the house, my stomach feeling like it was full of wriggling worms, my heart pounding. No matter how old I get, parents still freak me out!

Daniel led me into the living room, where his mother sat in an overstuffed armchair. The room was dimly lit, with late afternoon light peeking through the curtains. The television was turned off. His mother didn't seem to be reading or doing much of anything other than waiting. For me. My

stomach dropped. "She saw us kissing!" I thought, panicking. Or worse! "She knows my bag is full of condoms!"

But then his mother smiled wide, her eyes bright, and said the most fittingly bizarre greeting ever: "It's so nice to meet you. We have plenty of things for you to eat. I have meatless balls. With sauce!"

Clearly, the food thing had been just as much on her mind as it had been on mine. The week was pretty painless. His family was wonderful. Dan and I cooked a lot, the fridge was full of hummus and veggies and smoothie accoutrements, and nobody starved or got into a fist fight. Crisis averted!

Below are some tips for winning over your partner's omni fam, but first, a tip that has nothing to do with vegan-on-omni interaction, but a lot to do with likeability in general: be yourself. It's easy to spot a faker. Your stomach will tell you when someone isn't genuine. This has something to do with the gut being connected to the brain. Women especially have an uncanny ability to detect bullshit, so be extra real with mom. Unless you are genuinely kind of a dick. Then I don't know how to help you. Smile while you're being awful and hope everyone thinks you're joking?

A recipe for a winning 'Meet the Omnis' experience

One part good attitude. It doesn't matter how awkward you feel, or how much you wish you were at home where your mom always makes you a special side of smoky lentil pâté. Put on a smile. And some nice pants. If your partner has told their family you're vegan, they will probably have tried to accommodate you, as families do. But if not, and the meal is super meaty, put on a smile anyway. I hope you traveled with emergency hummus.

Two parts helpfulness. Once you've arrived at Family HQ, ask what you can do. Do it, and then ask what you can do again. Set the table, offer to make the stuffing (a sneaky way to veganize your fave dish), do the dishes. Cooking is the number one way you can ensure a positive eating experience—you will have something to munch, and you will have impressed everyone with your legendary caramelized Brussels sprouts. Another way you can be helpful—and your partner will thank you for this one—is to steer the conversation. Ask everyone questions. Everybody loves to talk about themselves. Plus, it will take some of the heat off of you, the outsider.

One part respect. Daniel's parents were cool with me sleeping in his bed whenever I visited. When his grandparents arrived for Thanksgiving one year, the third question out of his grandmother's mouth was, "And where are you sleeping?" I froze, eyes wide. Daniel was sitting right next to me, and I waited for him to pipe up. And waited. And waited. In retrospect, Daniel was never really good at social cues. After the moment had peaked into a nice awkward crescendo, I jabbed Dan in the ribs and he managed to cough up "she sleeps in my room." His grandmother digested that tidbit and then said, to Daniel, "And where do you sleep?" Once it was made clear we were bed buddies for the weekend, his grandmother excused herself and went right into the kitchen, where she most likely berated Dan's mom for allowing this premarital bedwarming. Ahhh, family. Daniel slept on the couch that weekend. The point is, whatever the rules are in the house you're visiting—follow them.

FOR SOME REASON, PEOPLE TAKE OTHER PEOPLE'S DIETARY PREFERENCES AS A CRITICISM OF THEIR OWN.

One part situational diffusion. Over the years, I have learned how to diffuse awkward or argumentative situations revolving around my veganism, like the time Dan's mom made me a special veg dish just for me—covered in cheese. It was still early on, and she didn't really understand the difference between vegan and vegetarian yet. Smile, be polite, stress how much you appreciate the effort and explain why you can't eat it. They feel just as awkward as you do. And then, there are the real awkward situations: the angry ones. For some reason, many people take other people's dietary preferences as a criticism of their own. When you're eating with a bunch of omnis you don't know, they will probably ask about your veganism. Depending on your explanation and the temperament of the folks you're with, they may even be offended. Choose your words carefully, don't focus on anyone's plate but your own, and if you must get into some of the graphic animal rights deets, suggest you talk more about it after the plates have been cleared. Remember you're a guest, and polite guests don't make little cousin Susie weep with a description of what really happens to Mr. Turkey.

AYINDÉ: Ginger and I divided the holiday season so we each got fam time. I had a choice between Thanksgiving or Kwanzaa. I chose Kwanzaa in Seattle with my folks. She got Thanksgiving in Cali with her folks. We got that discount ticket app out, bought tickets, and boom! We had "holiday plans" together as a couple.

Deep breath. Okay, this will be fine, I told myself. I'm the type of dude that the aunts, mothers, and grandmothers like. I don't know why, because I'm a bit of a rebel, vegan and all. Maybe it's because I can cook, or maybe I remind them of a dude they dated in their younger days. Not the dude they married, but the fun guy, you know....

Something to remember when meeting the family is that the holidays are an impress-fest, and you are showing that you have the potential to "settle down one day and have a family like your sister." Eye-roll. Despite your "crazy" vegan lifestyle or choices in "crazy" vegan mates, you brought someone home! That's huge. It hints that this one is a strong contender for "The One..." At least, if they have good manners and are polite, the parents will say "good enough!"

FAMILY DO'S AND DON'TS WITH AYINDÉ AND GINGER

Do: Be likeable. If you're a jerk by nature, suppress it with willpower. And alcohol. Or maybe avoid the alcohol. If you're a man trying to impress someone's father, remember that nothing is more respected than a self-made man or woman, so if you're an entrepreneur, play that card.

Don't: Vegans (this is for you): don't ask several times if this side dish they are offering you is vegan. You may come off as distrusting. As a life-long vegan, I have been slipped butter enough times to recognize it at first bite. Luckily, that wasn't an issue at Ginger's parents' home, once they got the word that I was not only a vegan but a professional chef.

Do: Practice table manners. Nothing can impress or intimidate people more than knowing your forks. Use your powers for good.

Don't: Miss this huge culinary opportunity to impress with the food. We know from the last chapter that you've been practicing your cooking skills, so put them through a semifinal at the Impress Fest. Speaking of cooking skills, let's get on with those holiday recipes.

"Be a thoughtful partner, period. Think about your partner's needs. This transcends simple diet and lifestyle aspects and into every corner of the relationship."
– BETH, OMNIVORE

A Very Special Dinner Menu

For when you need to throw an impress-fest

H oliday time! It's everyone's favorite time of year: family, friends, and awkward situations—you know it well. Sometimes, the only saving grace is the food! So let's make it good, shall we? In this chapter, I assembled a menu of seasonal holiday crowd pleasers. These work as both as individual entrees or as side dishes, so you can take them to a party on their own or put all these components together to make a grand feast. I believe in you! Feel free to dip back into the book and add some cornbread or biscuits to pull it all together.

Miso-Vermouth Braised Drunken Bok Choy

Prep time: 3 minutes | Cook time: 4 minutes | Serves 2 | GF, SF

At different points in my culinary career, I've gone through phases where I focus heavily on one type of food. An obsession, some might call it. I mentioned I went through a pickling phase. Well, at one point I was also braising everything. Bok choy is nutrient rich and naturally juicy, which makes it great for braising. Bok choy looks a little scary, like a cross between celery and spinach, so often people don't know if they're going to like it until you put it in front of them. In this recipe, miso adds pungent flavor and sets the dish off. I hope this is a beginning to your braising career. Braise on!

1 teaspoon chickpea miso

1/4 cup vermouth

1 tablespoon grapeseed or safflower oil

1/2 cup diced onion

3 stalks baby bok choy, cleaned, cut
    length wise

2 teaspoons dried thyme

1 teaspoon coarse salt

1. In a small bowl, combine the miso and vermouth, blending with a fork or whisk.

2. In a large skillet over medium-high heat, heat the oil until hot and shimmering. Add the onion and sauté until it begins to turn translucent, about 1 minute.

3. Add the bok choy, using tongs to turn and coat with oil. Add the thyme, salt, and vermouth and miso mixture. Reduce the heat to medium-low.

4. Cover the pan and allow to braise for 2 to 4 minutes. Remove from heat and keep covered for a few minutes until ready to serve. Serve hot.

WTF is braising, anyway? A little bit about braising: You have 2 kinds of heat when cooking—dry like in the oven or sautéing and wet like boiling or with water. When you braise, you use both. Dry heat is introduced to the liquid, and it begins to braise, creating a new level of flavor.

"*If you're in a serious relationship and see yourself having children together, make sure you're both on the same page regarding possible children's diets right off the bat. If not, that can make for a messy conversation later on.***"** – Graeme, VEGAN

White Mushroom Truffle Gravy

Prep time: 7 minutes | Cook time: 30 minutes | Serves 4

When brainstorming this recipe, I must have passed fifty emails back and forth with my then-editor at Veg-News Magazine. We were trying to land a gravy that you would literally want to drink. This gravy is sacred, and yes, it's good enough to drink. The mushrooms and truffle flavor blend the perfect amount of earthiness with a touch of sophistication. Trust me, you're gonna want to put it on just about anything. It's best paired with your holiday vegan centerpiece, whatever that may be. (Try some simple braised tempeh, page 79). Be sure to wipe your gravy mustache.

Note: Mixing a non-dairy milk with a lil' lemon juice is the oldest vegan cooking trick in the book. It creates something with a similar flavor to buttermilk. You're welcome.

1/4 cup vegan butter

2 tablespoons chopped onion

2 king oyster mushrooms, finely diced

1 1/2 teaspoons minced garlic

1 1/2 teaspoons minced fresh sage

1 1/2 teaspoons dried thyme

1 teaspoon chili powder

1/2 teaspoon freshly ground black pepper

1/2 tablespoon salt

2 tablespoons all-purpose flour

3 cups unsweetened soy milk, divided

1 tablespoon fresh lemon juice

1 teaspoon black truffle oil

1. Melt the butter in a large skillet over medium-high heat. Add the onion and mushrooms and sauté until the onion becomes translucent, 3 to 4 minutes.

2. Add garlic, sage, thyme, chili powder, pepper, and salt and sauté for 1 minute. Add flour and whisk until the flour is browned, 2 to 3 minutes.

3. In a small bowl, combine 1/2 cup of the soy milk with the lemon juice, then slowly add remaining soy milk. Add the soy-milk-lemon juice mixture to the skillet. Bring to a simmer, then reduce to medium-low heat. Whisk until smooth.

4. Add the truffle oil, reduce the heat to low, and cook for 15 to 20 minutes, stirring occasionally. Serve warm.

Granny's Candied Yams
with Marshmallows

Prep time: 7 minutes | Cook time: 60 minutes | Serves 4 to 6 | GF

One Easter at my maternal grandmother Pauline's house in Baltimore, fifteen-year-old Ayindé was offered this signature dish for the first time. It was an awkward moment as this wasn't a vegan option— at that time, vegan marshmallows were non-existent. "Oh it's just a little butter, baby," was her response to my mother's objection. Of course, granny was offended that I did not eat her food, and I was bummed because I thought it looked pretty good and like a clever combo; I wanted to eat it. Now that vegan marshmallows are a thing, I am able to revisit this recipe. This one is for you, Granny!

1 1/2 pounds sweet potatoes or yams, peeled and cut into 1-inch thick wheels

1 (14-ounce) can pineapple chunks, drained and 1/4 cup juice reserved

1/2 stick vegan butter, sliced, or 1/4 cup coconut oil (optional)

1 lemon, cut into 4 wedges

1/2 cup brown sugar

2 teaspoons ground cinnamon

1/4 teaspoon ground nutmeg

1/2 teaspoon salt

2 cups vegan marshmallows

1. Place the yam wheels into medium soup pot and cover with water. Bring to a boil over high heat, and cook the potatoes until fork tender, about 25 minutes. Pour off the water and let the potatoes drain and cool in a colander for 7 to 10 minutes. Preheat oven to 350°F.

2. Transfer the potatoes to a medium baking dish, and add the pineapple chunks and the 1/4 cup juice. Add the butter slices, if using, making sure they are evenly dispersed.

3. Place 1 wedge of lemon into each corner of the dish and sprinkle the brown sugar, cinnamon, nutmeg, and salt on top of the yams and pineapples. Bake for 15 minutes. Using oven mitt, remove from oven and evenly distribute the marshmallows on top. Return to oven and bake for another 15 minutes. Remove lemon wedges before serving.

Savory Shiitake and Parmesan Bread Pudding

Prep time: 10 minutes | Cook time: 30 minutes | Serves 4 to 6

Bread pudding is a staple in the Southern kitchen. It's often served as a breakfast or brunch dish, and can be either savory or sweet. This vegan version is savory. Because sometimes you have to indulge, this is not my healthiest dish. Indeed, it is plucked from the Paula Deen world. Be sure to pace yourself and enjoy!

3/4 cup + 2 tablespoons safflower oil, divided

1/2 cup chopped onion

1 tablespoon chopped garlic

1 1/2 cups sliced shiitake mushrooms

2 cups unsweetened soy milk

3/4 cup vegan Parmesan cheese

2 tablespoons nutritional yeast

2 tablespoons Ener-G egg replacer powder

1 tablespoon chopped fresh sage

1 teaspoon dried basil

1/2 teaspoon red pepper flakes

2 teaspoons salt

2 tablespoons nutritional yeast

3 cups bread, roughly torn apart into pieces (whatever kind you have)

1/4 cup chopped scallions, for garnish

1. Heat 2 tablespoons of oil in a skillet over medium-high heat, until hot. Add the onion and sauté until it becomes translucent, about 5 minutes. Add the garlic and shiitake mushrooms and cook, stirring, until softened, 3 minutes. Set aside. Preheat the oven to 350°F.

2. In large bowl, combine the soy milk, parmesan, nutritional yeast, egg replacer, sage, basil, red pepper flakes, and salt. With a handheld emulsion blender or in a high-speed blender, slowly blend 3/4 cup oil into the soy milk mixture until the consistency becomes thick and custard-like.

3. Fold in the sautéed mushrooms and onion. Add the bread pieces and fold together until well combined. Pour the mixture into a lightly oiled casserole dish and let it sit for 7 to 10 minutes. Bake for 30 minutes, or until hot. Serve garnished with chopped scallions.

5 THINGS YOU DIDN'T KNOW ABOUT SHIITAKES

1. In many cultures, shiitakes are viewed as a medicinal mushroom, which is NOT the same as a magic mushroom.

2. These little fungi are thought to support our immune system and protect us from cardiovascular disease.

3. Shiitakes are a great source of iron.

4. Shiitakes have grown wild since prehistoric times. They were chillin' with your friend the brontosaurus.

5. China currently produces over 80 percent of all commercially sold shiitake mushrooms.

Quinoa-Cranberry Wild Rice Skillet Stuffing

Prep time: 5 minutes | Cook time: 7 minutes | Serves 4 to 6 | GF, SFO

Ginger and I came up with this for a Thanksgiving we spent together during our move-to-Austin, start-a-quinoa-company fantasy period I mentioned earlier. The wild rice complements quinoa's nuttiness, and when paired with the cranberries, the dish is both savory and sweet. Still living in New York at the time, we were invited to Jersey for dinner and decided to bring this dish. Even though we were late, because we chose to have sex all morning, once at the dinner, everyone enjoyed our addition. Use soy-free Earth Balance to make this soy-free.

3 tablespoons vegan butter

1 cup chopped onion

1 cup chopped celery

2 tablespoons chopped fresh sage

1 tablespoon finely chopped fresh rosemary

1 teaspoon minced fresh thyme

2 cups cooked quinoa

1 cup cooked wild rice

1/2 cup dried cranberries

Salt and black pepper

1. Melt the butter in a large skillet over medium-high heat. Add the onion, celery, sage, rosemary, and thyme. Sauté until the onion becomes translucent, about 5 minutes.

2. Stir in the cooked quinoa, wild rice, and cranberries. Season with salt and pepper to taste. Mix well and sauté for 5 minutes or until hot.

WTF is so wild about wild rice? You might be surprised to learn that wild rice isn't even a grain, it's a grass. Yep, I'm telling you to go eat grass. Okay, technically it's a water-grass seed, and it was a staple in the diet of the Chippewa and Sioux Indian, so it's fitting to eat on Thanksgiving. Wild rice is also high in protein—roughly equivalent to quinoa, even! So munch on, grass eaters.

Truffle-Roasted Vegetable Medley

Prep time: 10 minutes | Cook time: 35 minutes | Serves 4 to 6 | GF, SF

In my later NYC years, I worked at a hippie-ish veggie joint in the Lower East Side of Manhattan. It was heavy on seasonal veggies, and we roasted a lot. They used things I would normally skip over, like turnips and squash. However, I learned to love them. They remind me of the simplicity of a garden and of eating seasonally. Your body needs certain things at different times of year, and in winter, you need roots to stay warm. This dish takes it all back to the basics. Just some oil, salt and pepper, heat, and a little added dill to finish. If you're not a dill fan, you can use your favorite herb to complement the veggies.

2 medium sweet potatoes or yams, cut into wedges

2 turnips, peeled and cut into wedges

1 butternut or other hard winter squash, halved, seeded, and cut into 1-inch slices

8 ounces baby carrots with stems

1 red onion, cut into wedges

3 tablespoons olive oil

Salt and black pepper

1/2 cup chopped dill

1 tablespoon black truffle oil, optional

1. Preheat the oven to 350°F. In a large bowl, combine all the vegetables. Add the olive oil and sprinkle with salt and pepper to taste, tossing to coat.

2. Place the oiled veggies on a lightly oiled baking sheet. Place in oven and roast until all the vegetables pieces are fork-tender.

3. Remove from the oven, top with fresh dill, and drizzle with truffle oil, if using. Serve hot.

"Separate pots, pans, and cutting boards. Or at least label one side of the cutting board as "vegan" and the other side as "what are you thinking?" – CLARK, VEGAN

Vodka Cranberry Sauce

Prep time: 3 minutes | Cook time: 10 minutes | Serves 4 to 6 | GF, SF

This is for the grown-up table at Thanksgiving. I couldn't help but pair these two: cranberry, the holiday season staple, and of course who doesn't like vodka? Put these two together to make a sauce, and it's heaven.

12 ounces fresh cranberries

1 cup granulated sugar

1/2 cup orange-flavored vodka

1/2 cup orange juice

1/2 teaspoon orange zest

Pinch of salt

1. In a small saucepan, combine the cranberries, sugar, vodka, orange juice, and orange zest, and bring to a boil.

2. Reduce the heat to low and cook until the cranberries burst, 8 to 10 minutes.

3. Continue to cook over very low heat until the desired consistency is reached. Add pinch of salt. Serve hot.

5 THINGS YOU DIDN'T KNOW ABOUT CRANBERRIES

1. On the antioxidant scale, the tart cranberry outranks nearly every other fruit and veggie, including spinach and broccoli. Damn!

2. In addition to being high in antioxidants, cranberries have natural antibacterial elements, which is why they're a common holistic cure for urinary tract infections.

3. We import the majority of our cranberries from other countries. Only five states in the U.S are heavy producers of cranberries: Wisconsin (the cranberry is their state fruit), Massachusetts, Oregon, New Jersey, and Washington.

4. Cranberries are one of only three native North American fruits currently cultivated, the others being blueberries and concord grapes. So maybe there's a reason we incorporate them heavily into our Thanksgiving dishes. Way to go, America.

5. At one point, cranberries were referred to as bear berries. Why? Because bears ate them. Yep.

Seitan Wellington, see next page

Seitan Wellington with Roasted Potatoes

Prep time: 45 minutes | Cook time: 50 minutes | Serves 4 to 6

Seitan is probably the most accessible protein for non-vegans. I chose a Wellington because it's based on a classic dish and presents very well. This recipe is not for the novice. I suggest you read it over several times before attempting. However, when done well and correctly, it is sure to please. The complex flavors and textures combine to create a meal that is both pleasing to the eye and filling to the stomach. Again, read through this recipe and be prepared like it's your mid-term and worth half your vegan grade.

Roasted Potatoes (page 272)

Green Peppercorn Sauce (page 272)

DUXELLES

2 cups button mushrooms

1/2 cup peeled, halved shallots

2 garlic cloves, crushed

2 teaspoon chopped fresh thyme

1 tablespoon vegan butter

1 tablespoon olive oil

Salt and black pepper

SEITAN BROTH

4 cups water

3 ribs celery, rough chopped

1/2 onion, quartered

2 tablespoons low-sodium wheat-free tamari

2 teaspoons salt

SEITAN

1 1/2 cups vital wheat gluten

1/4 cup nutritional yeast

1 tablespoon dried basil

2 teaspoons onion powder

1 teaspoon garlic powder

1 teaspoon smoked paprika

1 teaspoon gumbo filé powder (see page 25)

1 teaspoon salt

1 cup water

1 tablespoon safflower oil, plus more to sear seitan

2 tablespoons Dijon mustard

1 pound vegan puff pastry (Pepperidge Farm brand is vegan)

1. Prepare the roasted potatoes and green peppercorn sauce and set aside.

2. Duxelles: In a food processor, combine the mushrooms, shallots, garlic, and thyme. Pulse until pulverized. Melt the butter in a large skillet over medium-high heat, then add the olive oil. Add the shallots and mushroom mixture and sauté for approximately 10 minutes, or until most of the liquid has evaporated. Season with salt and pepper to taste. Set aside to cool.

3. Seitan Broth: Pour the water into a medium stockpot and bring to a boil. Add the celery, onion, tamari, and salt and keep at a low simmer while you prepare the seitan.

4. Seitan: In a medium bowl, combine the vital wheat gluten, nutritional yeast, basil, onion powder, garlic powder, smoked paprika, file powder, and salt.

5. Stir the water and oil into the dry ingredients and mix until it becomes a dough ball. The ball should be moist but not sticky. Knead the seitan ball together with your hands for exactly 2 minutes. Let your dough rest for 5 minutes.

6. Knead the seitan dough for another 2 minutes and let it rest for approximately 5 minutes. Using your hands, form the seitan into cylindrical shape, 8 to 10 inches long.

7. Bring the broth to a boil and place the seitan cylinder into the pot. Reduce heat to medium-low and simmer for approximately 7 minutes. Cook, uncovered, occasionally spooning broth over the top of the seitan. Remove the pot from the heat, and remove the seitan from broth. (Reserve the broth for the green peppercorn sauce.) Place the seitan on a cooling rack until it reaches room temperature. Preheat the oven to 425°F.

8. Once the seitan is cool, heat a thin layer of oil in a medium skillet over medium-high heat. Add the seitan and pan-sear it on all sides, then remove it from the pan to cool. Once cool, smear the Dijon mustard on the seitan and let it sit. Preheat the oven to 425°F.

9. Roll out the puff pastry. Spread the duxelles in center of the pastry, roughly the length of the seitan. Place the seitan in the center of the puff pastry on top of the duxelles mixture. Roll up the pastry and seitan until it is closed. Brush oil on the edge of the pastry to help seal it, tucking in the ends and sealing in the seitan.

10. Place the Wellington on a baking sheet, seam-side down. Brush the top with melted vegan butter and sprinkle with coarse sea salt. Make a couple of slits on the top of the puff pastry to create steam vents. Bake for 30 to 35 minutes. About 10 minutes before the Wellington is done baking, return the potatoes to the oven so they're nice and toasty for serving.

11. To serve, transfer the Wellington to a cutting board. Use a serrated knife to cut it into 1/2-inch thick slices. Serve hot with the potatoes and the green peppercorn sauce on the side.

Pro-Tip: Flambé is a means to burn off alcohol to leave you with the flavor of the sprits or wine you are using, in this case brandy. The flames are finite; they will disappear after the initial burn. When you light it, be sure to have space above and no low-hanging flammable things like hair or weave and just let it burn—it usually takes about 20 seconds.

Roasted Potatoes

2 pints fingerling potatoes, scrubbed (3 1/2 to 4 cups)

2 tablespoons chopped fresh rosemary

1 tablespoon chopped fresh sage

3 tablespoons safflower oil

Salt and black pepper

6 cloves garlic, unpeeled

Preheat the oven to 450°F. In a medium bowl, combine the potatoes, rosemary, sage, oil, and salt and pepper to taste. Toss to coat. Transfer the potatoes to a baking sheet. Place the garlic cloves around the potatoes. Bake until tender, approximately 25 minutes. Remove from the oven and set aside.

Green Peppercorn Sauce

1 1/2 cups water

1 cup soaked cashews

2 tablespoons fresh lemon juice

2 tablespoons vegan butter

1/2 cup sliced shallots

1 teaspoon minced garlic

1 teaspoon minced fresh thyme

1/3 cup brandy

1 cup remaining seitan broth

2 tablespoons Dijon mustard

1/3 cup green peppercorns

Salt and white pepper

1. In a blender, combine the cashews and water and blend until smooth. Add the lemon juice and blend again. The mixture should thicken and coagulate once the lemon is added. Transfer the cream to a bowl and set aside.

2. In a medium skillet over medium-high heat, melt the butter. Add the shallots and sauté for approximately 2 minutes. Add the garlic and thyme and sauté 1 minute longer.

3. Add the brandy, then remove from the heat. Flambé the brandy using a kitchen match. Once the brandy burns out, place the skillet back over medium heat. Add the seitan broth, stirring to combine.

4. Stir in the reserved cashew cream and lower the heat to medium-low. Cook, stirring, until the sauce reduces by half, about 20 minutes Add the mustard and green peppercorns and season with salt and white pepper to taste. Remove from the heat.

WTF is duxelles? Duxelles is a fancy way of saying "mushroom mixture." Traditionally, it's a blend of minced mushrooms, onions, and herbs sautéed in butter and then reduced to a paste. Look at you, you're learning to make duxelles. Make sure to tell all of your co-workers that's what you did this weekend...

Stories from the Field

Chloé Jo Davis, founder of Girlie Girl Army

"My husband told me on our first date not to try and turn him into a vegetarian. Then he watched *Peaceable Kingdom* and went vegan that day. I saw a big heart in him and knew that if he'd read what I read and seen what I'd seen, he would make the change. Here we are, both vegan and together eight years with two human kids and five rescued pets. You can't go deep, real, dirty, and forever with someone who doesn't have the same wide expanse of heart that you do. And by "wide expanse," I mean selfless enough to give up the ego of eating animals for the greater good of compassion, the Earth, reverence for life, and self."

6. COHABITATION

"No, it's nothing like a 24-hour slumber party..."

It's always funny when the reality of living with someone sets in. It's usually when you need space and realize that the best you can do is hide out in the bathroom. Pretty soon, you're sulking on a closed toilet seat and letting the tap water run as a cover while your live-in is thinking "Damn, they must have some pretty clean teeth by now."

AYINDÉ: Ginger and I never really lived together, but a year and a half in, it felt like we did. You know, stuff at each other's places, sleeping together every night, that kind of thing. One morning, we had a serious conversation about moving in together. I launched into a rant about how, if we shack up, I was not having any meat in my house. She agreed to that stipulation. Feeling in charge, I took it a step further and said "And you gotta be vegan!" She responded with "I'll be vegan...at the house."

See, she was compromising. I, on the other hand, was not. I pushed further. "What do you mean 'at the house'? I want vegan babies one day!"

After that, the conversation changed sharply. She accused me of trying to control her. She wanted to know what right I had to tell her that she can't feed the (hypothetical) child she carried for nine months "real" ice cream. It was then that she finally laid it out: she would never really be vegan, because she didn't fundamentally believe in it. Things escalated from there. It was one of those calm matter-of-fact arguments that ended with her asking me a simple question: "So if I eat some chicken, you're gonna break up with me?" To that I replied, "Yes." She said alright. It seemed, to me, that we had reached some sort of agreement. That I had won!

Feeling like some progress had been made, I got up and went shopping for dinner. Upon my return, I smelled a familiar scent that I couldn't quite place. I walked into the place all "Hey babe, you won't believe the deal got on the quinoa..." I turned the corner to find Ginger eating out of a box with Fried Chicken printed on it. Truth.

She said, between lip-smacking, "So, are you going to break up with me now?"

Things got really, well, real, as I quickly processed her action. She was not only eating that yard bird, but simultaneously feeding me my words. Compromise was staring me in the face, and I had to ask myself a question, and fast: did I love this woman more than what she eats? The answer was yes. Followed by the thought, "You may have won this battle, my dear, but the war has just begun..."

Joking. I learned quickly that when you're unwilling to compromise, you immediately start a power struggle, and someone has to win. I had basically opened up the resentment bank and made a huge first deposit.

I might as well tell you about the only time in my life I have ever cooked meat. It was for Ginger, on our anniversary. We still didn't officially live together, and by this time, we had had more than a couple of heated discussions about being vegan and cohabiting. So it was becoming the elephant in the room at the dinner table with us as well. Luckily elephants are also vegan so he was on my side.

As our anniversary neared, we were both over the constant divide at the dinner table, and I was at my wits' end. I asked my sister for advice and she said, "Cook her some fish." I was like "Huh?" She said "Yeah, show her you love her just the way she is."

So I went to Whole Foods. I circled the store debating, if I could do this. "What if someone sees me buying meat?!" I wondered. I'd be ousted as a fraud! Then there was also the realization that I had literally never cooked meat before. My sister said to buy something white and cook it like tempeh. I don't remember the "kind," but I got it and paid like $5.00 a pound (and my pound of tempeh was $1.99, you do the math).

THERE SHOULD BE SOME AGREED-UPON RULES, PREFERABLY MADE BEFORE THE COHABBING BEGINS.

I came home and rushed around, trying to work fast and keep everything completely separate. Two containers of marinade, two cooking utensils, two of everything. It was crazy. When I finally got it done and served it to Ginger, she couldn't believe it. She said, "This looks just like fish!" After I told her, the look in her eyes changed, and well, the term "best sex ever" comes rushing to mind. Unfortunately, from the gesture came two different sets of expectations, neither of which was on point. My thought was, "Yes, I love you for who you are. Now please change." Her thought was, "Well, I finally put that to bed. Score one, Ginger."

ZOË: A year after college graduation, I was working for a small start-up company in Virginia, and Dan was finishing up a five-month internship on the West Coast. Not that I was keeping track or anything, but it had been roughly 154 days since we had done more than video chat, and so you can imagine the emotional recipe I concocted when Dan's company offered him a permanent position in California. It went a little something like this: One part "That's Great Honey," two parts "I'm Really Sick of Masturbating," shaken and served over ice. It was a very conflicted emotional beverage.

In the end, Daniel decided he would turn down the job if it meant heading back down south, applying to grad school, and shacking up with me. At first, I was thrilled with this solution. I had never lived with anyone in a romantic sense, and I didn't think it would be such a big deal. I mean,

I'd had tons of roommates before. In college, I had twelve roommates, and an unofficial one who slept on the couch and stored her clothes behind the entertainment center. Plus, Dan and I had had slumber parties all the time in college. Literally every night. Wouldn't it be just like that? An extended slumber party? Wouldn't I just be giving him a permanent place to store his toothbrush? Keep dreamin', sweet cheeks...

As Daniel and I started making plans to move in together, I began to think more and more about the ways our differences might collide, and wondered what our biggest issues might be. I'm the type of person who likes to be well-prepared. It's harder to trip over well-laid foundation. With that in mind, I asked Dan the most difficult thing about dating a vegan. The words were barely out of my mouth before he offered an enthusiastic one-word reply:

"Cheese."

Cheese? That's it? Not the sheath of awkwardness that cloaks me at any food-centric social gathering? Not the issue of choosing a restaurant together, or my refusal to share movie theater pop-

corn? Not the way I wrinkle my nose after you've eaten a hot dog? I pressed him for more.

"I just want to put cheese on everything. Like that time we made enchiladas, I was thinking, 'Oh, but these would be so much better with a little bit of cheese....'"

You ask any vegetarian why they aren't vegan, and they will tell you it's because of cheese. Really, do it. I dare you. "Oh, but I could never stop eating cheese..." is the number one I Could Never Be Vegan reason ever invented. And believe me, I get it. During the ten years I was a vegetarian, my love affair with cheese was borderline psychotic, especially when you consider that I'm lactose intolerant. Cheese was making me ill, but I still couldn't stop eating it. It hurt so good!

Well-prepared dishes—vegan or other—will not be lacking in flavor. However, cheese clearly weighed high on Daniel's "Things I Don't Want to Live Without" roster, second only to me, of course. Once we moved in together, a bag of shredded dairy cheese for sprinkling on his meals was the main non-vegan thing Daniel kept in the house. Cheese was our compromise. It may have been one of the only things we compromised on. I'm an Aries, okay? I only know one way to do things. (Mine.)

So if you're about to make your household a divided one, figure out the logistics of the vegan/omni food situation before you start packing up your Batman memorabilia for the move.

Guidelines for happy cohabiting

Here are a few do's and don'ts to help you out—and good freakin' luck.

AYINDÉ: Do set rules

There should be some agreed-upon rules, preferably made before the cohabbing begins. You must think of the most important thing to you, and use other considerations as bargaining chips. It's all about negotiation. So, vegan, if yours is "no meat in the house" or "dairy is cool but no flesh," then decide and push for it. Omni, yours may be "no way will I feel like a stranger in my own fridge!" Or maybe you're fine with eating veg at home but once you're out on the town, all is fair game. Vegan, you can take solace in the fact that it's still a bad economy so most meals will be eaten at home anyway. Win!

ZOË: Do work out a grocery plan

Shared expenses are something that every cohabbing couple needs to address, but it becomes a bit trickier when it's a vegan-on-omni pair. Freshly relocated, Daniel was looking for work when we first moved in together, and we were on a pretty tight budget. We decided the easiest way to

navigate food was to alternate the grocery tabs. One week, I pay, the next week, he does. Sounds easy, right? However, the problem was that Daniel would eat everything I ate—tempeh, farro, flax, you name it. If I brought it home, he would eat it. So while Daniel got down on everything regardless of who purchased what, our method would result in my paying for Dan's dairy, which I didn't agree with. Eventually we decided we could still alternate grocery bills, but Daniel would always pay for his own dairy. I also asked that he bought his own junk food, since I was less apt to binge on potato chips and sugary cereals. Figure out what works for your coupleship specifically, and navigate from there.

AYINDÉ: Don't cross-contaminate

In the restaurant world, like in homes, there is such a thing as cross-contamination. This is something to keep in mind of you are going for a separate-but-equal vegan/omni kitchen. Example: you stack a plate of meat on top of vegetables and the blood drips on the veggies and everyone gets salmonella and dies. No seriously, keep your food separate even when you're tired. (I'm looking at you, omni.) I know it's home, and you're extra lazy at home, so somebody might forget that the kale salad was cut with the same knife used on a piece of cheese, but for vegans, that can be a problem! Color coding works well to solve this. Pick a color for veg-only knives, cutting boards, pots and pans, etc.

ZOË: Do create safe spaces.

Daniel and I didn't color code, but we did create some completely vegan spaces emblazoned with the words "meat and dairy, thou shalt never trespass!" Shakespeare said that, I think. This helps you avoid repetitive fights about who stuck their wedge of cheddar in the veggie crisper. Have a vegan shelf in the fridge, a vegan shelf in the cupboard, and vegan pots, pans, cutting boards, etc.

AYINDÉ: Don't move in together if you can't afford enough space!

Studio apartments and tiny one-bedroom living is crazy tough on the "I want-to-be-by-myself-ophiles." Not to mention ventilation. That morning fried-egg smell you agreed to can be shocking to some vegans, and even tempting to others, so be prepared. Oh, and god forbid, turkey! Turkey bacon in your own skillet was a win for you, omni, but that tryptophan is hard to deal with. Trust me, the vegan will have words about this, so be prepared. I had to full-on leave the house once when my Auntie was making Thanksgiving dinner. I came in with a horrified look on my face, like "What is that?" Here's a little tip that goes well beyond cohabitation: Never make that face and combine those words when any woman is cooking.

ZOË: Do cook together.

You may think that because your diets are separate, you can't cook together. This is heart-breaking! Please cook together as often as possible. Not only is it bonding, but cooking vegan grub for your omni or tasting your vegan's version of gumbo can open up your palate and show you that food is still delicious when not cooked in bacon grease or smothered in cheese. Omni: veganize some of your favorites, pore through some great vegan cookbooks (cough, this one, cough), and have fun with it. Daniel and I loved cooking together, and most of my best memories of our relationship during cohabitation took place in the kitchen. I don't know what that says about our sex life, but...kidding! I'm kidding.

AYINDÉ: Do be responsible.

If you, vegan, fought for the right to a vegan kitchen, you better be cooking your ass off. Omni, if you agreed not to cross-contaminate, don't slice your brie on the veggie board when you're home alone. You two owe it to each other to stick to your word! You're partners now. I dated a woman once whose last boyfriend had a severe nut allergy, but she loved PB&J sandwiches! She couldn't have them in the house, and couldn't even eat them outside if she wanted to kiss him later. She had this whole routine of how to get PB&Js on the black market, and then floss and gargle like crazy so he wouldn't go into anaphylactic shock and die. While you won't accidentally murder your vegan hottie with burger breath, they will keep their distance from you for a while, and this whole vegan vs. non-vegan thing is a friggin' powder keg anyway, so choose your battles.

ZOË: Don't be anal.

When it comes to your living situation, you can't be too tight. You can set up guidelines, and boundaries, and an entire vegan cupboard, but every now and then somebody is gonna get sloppy and drain their bacon grease over the vegan pots and pans sitting in the sink. Take a breath, remember you're both human, and try not to throw any cutlery.

Stories from the Field

JL Fields, author and founder of JL Goes Vegan

"I went vegetarian, and later vegan, years after getting married. When I went vegetarian, I was in Kenya and had a sad experience with a goat. I called my husband and told him I was going vegetarian. Dave did most of the cooking at that time in our marriage, so he took it upon himself to figure out how to make vegetarian meals. Eight years later, I went vegan, and it was time for me to step it up in the kitchen. He respects my decision to live a vegan life and is incredibly supportive. We set boundaries right away. I declared that I would not buy animal products, or prepare foods with them, and he was fine with that. If he wants it, he buys it and cooks it. It worked. I would say that, early on, the challenges involved social situations. I think he was a bit uncomfortable with my insistence about choosing veg-friendly restaurants when dining out with others or serving only vegan food when people came over. But, as with all new things, it gets easier over time. These days he is vegetarian at home—his choice—and, frankly, makes the majority of our vegan meals. And he is the one who now insists that we find restaurants that will serve me "more than grilled vegetables.''

Recipes for Cohabitation

Cook like you mean it

"*I won't cook meat and my husband doesn't cook. So what he gets for dinner is up to me, and he's never complained.***"** – LYDIA, VEGAN

Moroccan Tempeh Chermoula

Prep time: 10 minutes | Cook time: 35 minutes | Serves 2

My first pop-up in NYC was with Joshua Katcher. It was called The Gracious Gourmand in a small place in Williamsburg, Brooklyn. For my night, I wanted to explore the Mediterranean from Italy to Spain, and we landed in Morocco for the main dish. I love intricate flavors like this—the more complex, the better. This sauce is easy to make and lasts a long time in the fridge. Served over couscous, the flavor will transport you right to Casablanca.

8 ounces tempeh

CHERMOULA

1/2 cup extra-virgin olive oil

1/4 cup chopped fresh parsley

1/4 cup chopped fresh cilantro

1/4 cup lemon juice

2 tablespoons chopped fresh mint

1 tablespoon smoked paprika

1/2 teaspoon minced garlic

1/2 teaspoon lemon zest

1/2 teaspoon salt

COUSCOUS

2 3/4 cups water

1/4 teaspoon salt

1 1/2 cup couscous

1. Tempeh: Cut the tempeh crosswise into 1/8-inch thick pieces and follow the cooking instructions on page 79 until the tempeh is fully cooked and flavorful. Set aside. Reserve the braising liquid.

2. Chermoula: Combine all the chermoula sauce ingredients in a blender and blend until the consistency is well-mixed but chunky. Set aside.

3. Couscous: Bring the water to a boil in a saucepan. Stir in the salt, then add the couscous and remove from the heat. Cover and set aside for about 5 minutes. The couscous should be light and fluffy, not gummy. Be sure to allow the couscous enough time to absorb the water.

4. In a medium skillet over medium-high heat, pan-sear the tempeh for about 2 minutes on each side. Repeat until all the tempeh is pan-seared. Set aside.

5. Plating: Working quickly, scoop about 1/4 cup of warm couscous on the center of each plate. Top with hot tempeh. Use a ladle or large spoon to spoon some of the braising liquid over the tempeh and couscous. Finally, spoon about 2 tablespoons of the chermoula sauce over the tempeh. Serve with extra sauce on the table with a communal spoon.

Cajun Tofu with Dirty Quinoa

Prep time: 10 minutes | Cook time: 30 minutes | Serves 2 | GF

Every now and then, I get lazy and hit the easy button. Often, this includes falling on my favorite prepared spice staple: Cajun seasoning. This rub is a nice blend of salt and red spices that can act as the undertone or the main flavor. In this recipe, it's the main flavor. Traditionally, dirty rice is made with meat, rice, and herbs. I stripped it down to the main flavors and switched the rice to quinoa for extra protein. It is an flavorful dish guaranteed to satisfy.

QUINOA

2 cups water

1 cup quinoa, well-rinsed

1 tablespoon grapeseed or safflower oil

1 tablespoon vegan butter

1/2 cup finely chopped onion

1/2 cup finely chopped celery

1/2 cup chopped bell pepper

1 teaspoon minced garlic

2 tablespoons low-sodium wheat-free tamari

1 tablespoon Cajun seasoning

1 teaspoon minced fresh thyme

1/4 teaspoon red pepper flakes (optional)

Sea salt

TOFU

8 ounces extra-firm tofu, frozen and defrosted

2 tablespoons Cajun seasoning

1 teaspoon dried basil

1/2 teaspoon dried thyme

1/2 teaspoon garlic powder

1/2 teaspoon onion powder

1/2 teaspoon dried sage

1 tablespoon safflower oil

1/4 cup water

2 tablespoons low-sodium wheat-free tamari

BUTTER SAUCE

1 tablespoon vegan butter

2 tablespoons finely chopped onion

1 tablespoon Cajun seasoning

1 teaspoon dried basil

1 teaspoon chopped fresh sage

1/2 cup dry white wine (see Pro-Tip), divided

1/2 teaspoon cornstarch

GARNISH

1/4 cup sliced cherry tomatoes, sliced

1. **Quinoa:** In a saucepan, bring the water to a boil, then stir in the quinoa. Reduce the heat to medium-low, cover, and cook until the water is absorbed, 10 to 15 minutes. Be careful not to overcook. Set aside.

2. In a large skillet over medium-high heat, heat the oil and butter. Add the onion, celery, and bell pepper and sauté for 3 to 5 minutes, stirring constantly from the bottom of the pan to prevent sticking. Add the garlic, and sauté for an additional minute.

3. Add the cooked quinoa and mix well. Add the tamari, Cajun seasoning, thyme, and red pepper flakes (if using), and mix until all ingredients are well-incorporated. Remove from the heat.

4. **Tofu:** Cut the tofu into 4 slices, approximately 1/8-inch thick. Use a paper towel to press out as much water from the tofu as possible, then transfer the tofu to a shallow bowl. In a separate small bowl combine Cajun seasoning, basil, thyme, garlic powder, onion powder, and sage and mix well. Use your hands to gently rub the seasoning mixture onto the tofu, coating well. Set aside.

5. Heat the oil in a medium skillet over medium heat. Add the tofu and sear for 3 minutes on each side, until brown and slightly crispy. Add the water and tamari to the skillet and allow to reduce for 3 to 5 minutes. Spoon about 1/4 cup of the dirty quinoa onto the plates and top with the tofu.

6. Butter Sauce: Melt the butter in a medium skillet over high heat. Add the onion and sauté for 30 to 45 seconds. Add the Cajun seasoning, basil, and sage. Working quickly, add 1/4 cup of the white wine and the cornstarch and sauté until mixture begins to bubble rapidly. Mix continually with a whisk or fork. Add the remaining 1/4 cup of white wine and allow the alcohol to burn off. It may flambé, but the fire won't last long. Remove from the heat and stir until the sauce becomes cloudy. Immediately spoon the butter sauce over the plated quinoa and tofu and garnish with sliced grape tomatoes.

Pro-Tip: Wine-butter sauce is meant to carry the flavor from the main dish through with a bit of fat and an extra fermented flavor of wine. Obviously, the better the quality of wine, the better the sauce, but don't be scared to use some Two-Buck Chuck.

WTF is the big deal about quinoa? A couple of years ago, quinoa blew up in popularity. It went from hanging on the back shelf of the health food store to headlining the A-list at every party. Nowadays, quinoa can't even step out of the house without being bombed by the paparazzi. However, there is merit behind the madness. Quinoa is actually a seed, not a grain, and is beloved by vegans because unlike many other plant sources, it is a complete protein. It is also extremely high in antioxidants and phytonutrients. To avoid commonly-used pesticides, choose organic.

Fillet de Soy with Blood Orange-Napa Cabbage Slaw

Prep time: 20 minutes | Cook time: 10 minutes | Serves 2 | GF

This recipe is inspired by Nobuyuki "Nobu" Matsuhisa. While touring with India.Arie, some friends and I took a night off to have dinner at Nobu. Everyone was enjoying their sashimi and sushi, and I was pleasantly surprised that my tofu steak was perfection! I have always loved tofu steak, but never expected it to be so good at a non-vegan establishment. They put so much time and care into making it, and I was really impressed. This rendition is more of an impress-your-mate type of meal, complete with a butter sauce, pickled greens, and a fat tofu steak.

COLESLAW

2 1/4 cups shredded Napa cabbage

1 tablespoon orange zest

1 teaspoon sugar

Juice of 1/2 blood orange (about 2 tablespoons)

1 teaspoon salt

MARINADE

1/4 cup water

2 tablespoons low-sodium wheat-free tamari

1 teaspoon chopped fresh sage

1 teaspoon nutritional yeast

1 teaspoon chopped garlic

1/2 teaspoon chopped fresh thyme

1/2 teaspoon chili powder

1/4 teaspoon white pepper

TOFU

1 tablespoon grapeseed or safflower oil

8 ounces firm tofu, frozen and defrosted, sliced
    into 2-inch squares, 1/2 inch thick

1/2 medium onion, cut into rings

SAUCE

2 tablespoons vegan butter, divided

1 tablespoon chopped chives

Salt and black pepper

1 teaspoon cornstarch mixed with 2 tablespoons
    water

1 tablespoon orange juice

3 tablespoons red wine

1. **Coleslaw:** In a bowl, combine the cabbage, orange zest, and sugar. Mix well and set aside until the tofu is ready to serve. (Just before serving, add the orange juice and salt and mix well. This will preserve the crunch factor.)

2. **Marinade:** In a shallow bowl, combine the marinade ingredients and set aside.

3. **Tofu:** Heat the oil in a skillet over medium-high heat. Add the tofu and pan-sear it on both sides until golden brown, 3 to 4 minutes per side. Be careful not to let it burn. Add the onion rings to the skillet and sauté for 1 minute.

4. Reduce the heat to medium. Add the marinade to the pan. Cover and braise over medium-low heat for 3 minutes. Reduce the heat to low and simmer until the marinade evaporates. Remove from the heat.

5. **Plating:** While the tofu braises, start building the plate. Add the salt and orange juice to the slaw and mix well. Spoon approximately 4 ounces of coleslaw on each plate, just off-center. Once the tofu is ready, place

the hot tofu steaks in the center of each plate. Top with the onions and, using the same pan, start your butter sauce.

6. Sauce: Using the same skillet, melt 1 tablespoon vegan butter over high heat. Add the chives, lower the heat to medium-high and sauté for 30 to 45 seconds. Add dash of salt and pepper.

7. Add the cornstarch and water mixture to the pan, along with the orange juice. Stir until the mixture begins to simmer rapidly. Add the red wine. As the alcohol burns off quickly, you may see a small flame. It will go away very fast. Don't panic—it's called a flambé. Remove the pan from the heat and add the remaining tablespoon of butter. Stir until all ingredients are well-incorporated. Pour the sauce over the plated tofu steaks and serve immediately

Seitan Kebabs
with Sangria Tomato Salad

Prep time: 25 minutes | Cook time: 25 minutes | Serves 2 to 4

Quickie Two was the name of the restaurant I grew up in, a little vegan spot in the middle of the hood run by my parents and a few neighborhood kids who needed jobs. After I was grown and out of the house, I came home to visit one summer and was asked to revamp the menu. One idea I had was kebabs, inspired by my time in Manhattan and the infamous meat-on-a-stick vendors. I thought, how could I make this vegan? Seitan is a complete protein with the mouthfeel of meat, so I went with that. Truthfully, it was the marinade that made the kebabs a hit. The tomato salad came from my experience with house parties and a thing called spootie, which is basically a bunch of fruit soaked in liquor overnight. Sangria on steroids is really what it's like. I reinvented it with white wine and cherry tomatoes to make a savory salad. You will need 6 to 8 wooden or metal skewers for this recipe. If using wooden skewers, soak them in water for about 20 minutes before using.

SALAD

2 cups sliced cherry tomatoes

1/4 cup julienned red onion

1/2 cup diced English cucumber

2 teaspoons dried basil

2 tablespoons olive oil

1 teaspoon sea salt

1/2 cup dry white wine

MARINADE

1/2 cup olive oil

1/3 cup lemon juice

1/4 cup vegan Worcestershire sauce

2 tablespoons dried basil

1 tablespoon dried parsley

2 teaspoons minced garlic

1/2 teaspoon ground white pepper

1/2 teaspoon sea salt

KEBABS

1 yellow bell pepper, cut into large
   pieces

1 green bell pepper, cut into large
   pieces

1 red onion, cut into large pieces

6 to 8 button mushrooms (optional)

1 pound seitan, cut into chunks

1. Salad: Mix all salad ingredients together in a small bowl. Set aside for 15 to 20 minutes while making the kebabs.

2. Marinade: Mix all marinade ingredients together in a shallow baking dish large enough to hold the skewers. Set aside.

3. Kebabs: Slide a piece of onion, pepper, mushroom (if using), and seitan onto each skewer, repeating until the skewers are full, leaving 1/2 inch free at either end.

4. Place the skewers in the marinade and set aside for 25 to 30 minutes, turning occasionally.

5. Preheat a lightly-oiled stovetop griddle. Arrange the skewers on the hot griddle and grill until the vegetables are tender and browned all over, 5 to 7 minutes. Serve hot with the salad on the side.

Bibimbap

Prep time: 8 minutes | Cook time: 7 minutes | Serves 2 | GF

I went on a couple of dates with a Korean woman, let's call her Sochi, and she told me that in actuality, it's very rare to find vegan Chinese food. She told me that Chinese restaurants lie to us Americans so that we order their food, which usually has fish sauce or some other hidden animal ingredient. Well, great. Anyway, we went to a Korean restaurant and I thought I was safe ordering bibimbap. I double-checked with the waiter to make sure. I really enjoyed it, so much that I took a supermarket trip down the international aisle to remake it. I am still suspicious of all Chinese food. Thanks, Sochi.

1/4 cup toasted sesame oil

2 tablespoons low-sodium wheat-free tamari

2 tablespoons brown sugar

3/4 tablespoon gochujang hot chili paste

2 teaspoons rice vinegar

1 teaspoon minced garlic

2 tablespoons grapeseed or safflower oil

8 ounces tofu, cut into four equal slices

2 cups sliced shiitake or button mushrooms (optional)

2 cups cooked basmati rice

2 cups baby spinach

1 cup shredded carrots

1 cup bean sprouts

1 cup sliced red onion

2 cups cooked basmati rice

Toasted sesame seeds, for garnish

1. In a small bowl, combine the sesame oil, tamari, sugar, chili paste, vinegar, and garlic. Mix well and set aside.

2. Heat the oil in a skillet over medium-high heat. Add the tofu and cook until browned on both sides, about 5 minutes. If using mushrooms, add them in at this point. Add half of the reserved sauce mixture. Reduce the heat to medium-low, cover, and cook for 3 to 5 minutes. Remove from the heat.

3. Divide the cooked rice between two bowls. Evenly divide the spinach, carrots, bean sprouts, and onion between the bowls, scattering them on top of the rice. (The vegetables remain raw.)

4. Top with the tofu. Sprinkle with toasted sesame seeds and drizzle the remaining sauce on top.

Crispy Seitan Parmesan

Prep time: 15 minutes | Cook time: 30 minutes (plus time to make seitan) | Serve 4 to 6

When I used to work as a bartender in a pizza restaurant in my early NYC days, we sold a lot of chicken Parmesan. I thought it would be easy to recreate, so I came up with a version for my parents' café in Tacoma, Washington. I changed the sauce to a lighter tomato version that you can create using ingredients already in your kitchen. This is a hearty dish that satisfies both the vegan and omnivore, creating a peaceful atmosphere at the table.

Pro-Tip: Make the seitan a day or two ahead and store it in the fridge to cut way down on the prep time. (See photo on page 144.)

TOMATO SAUCE

1 tablespoon safflower oil

1 tablespoon chopped fresh basil

1 tablespoon dried oregano

1 teaspoon minced garlic

2 cups quartered fresh tomatoes

Salt

2 tablespoons olive oil

SEITAN BROTH

6 cups water

3 ribs celery, rough chopped

1/2 onion, quartered

2 tablespoons low-sodium wheat-free tamari

2 teaspoons salt

SEITAN

2 cups vital wheat gluten

1/4 cup chickpea flour

1/4 cup nutritional yeast

1/2 tablespoon dried basil

1 tablespoon dry thyme

2 teaspoons onion powder

1 teaspoon garlic powder

1 teaspoon smoked paprika

1 teaspoon dried sage

1 teaspoon salt

1/4 teaspoon celery seed

1 cup water

1 tablespoon grapeseed or safflower oil

NOODLES

12 ounces fettuccine noodles

Salt and olive oil

BREADING

1 cup all-purpose flour

1/2 cup panko bread crumbs

1 teaspoon paprika

1 teaspoon salt

1 teaspoon black pepper

1 cup soy milk, for dredging

1 cup safflower oil, for frying

1 cup shredded vegan mozzarella

1/2 cup vegan Parmesan

1. **Tomato Sauce:** Place the tomatoes in a food processor and pulse until roughly chopped. Set aside.

2. Heat 1 tablespoon oil in a medium saucepan over medium heat Add the basil, oregano, and garlic and sauté for 45 seconds. Be careful not to burn. Add the tomatoes to the saucepan. Reduce the heat to medium-low. Season with salt to taste, stir in the olive oil, remove from the heat, and set aside.

3. **Seitan Broth:** In a medium stockpot, bring the water to a boil. Add the celery, onion, tamari, and salt and reduce to a low simmer.

4. Seitan: In a medium bowl, combine the vital wheat gluten, chickpea flour, nutritional yeast, thyme, onion powder, garlic powder, smoked paprika, sage, salt, and celery seed. Stir the water and oil into the dry ingredients and mix until it becomes a dough ball. The ball should be moist, but not sticky. Knead the seitan ball with your hands for approximately 2 minutes. Let the dough rest for 5 minutes. Knead the dough for another 2 minutes and let it rest for approximately 5 minutes. Bring the broth back up to a boil.

5. Cut the seitan into three equal pieces and drop into the boiling broth. Reduce the heat to a simmer, cover, and cook for approximately 35 minutes. The seitan will double in size. Allow to cool, then cut the seitan into cutlets. Set aside.

6. Noodles: Bring 4 cups of water to a boil in a medium stockpot. Add 1 tablespoon salt and 2 tablespoons oil. Add the noodles and cook until al dente, 10 to 12 minutes, or according to package directions. Drain the hot water from the noodles and return the noodles to the pot. Cover and keep warm until ready to serve.

7. Breading: In a shallow pan, combine the flour, panko, paprika, salt, and pepper. Mix well. Pour in the milk into a separate shallow pan. One at a time, dip the seitan cutlets in the milk coating, both sides. Transfer to the breading mixture, coating both sides. Repeat so each cutlet is double-coated. Place the cutlets on parchment paper and set aside until the cutlets are moist to the touch, approximately 7 minutes.

8. Preheat the broiler. Heat the oil in a medium skillet over medium-high heat until hot. Carefully place the cutlets into the hot oil, cooking both sides until golden brown, about 3 minutes per side. Remove the cutlets from the oil with tongs or a spatula and place on paper towels to drain excess oil.

9. Transfer the cutlets to a baking sheet and sprinkle them with the vegan mozzarella and Parmesan. Place under the broiler for approximately 5 to 7 minutes, or until the cheese has melted and seitan is golden and crispy. Serve over the noodles with the tomato sauce.

"I tried to learn more about veganism and learn more recipes that I could make my vegan girlfriend. She has definitely influenced my eating habits since we've been together and as time goes on, I slowly try more and more vegan dinners with her." – Joe, omnivore

Stories from the Field

Leanne Mai-ly Hilgart, founder of Vaute Couture

"Derek had walked in my store when we first opened, though we didn't meet until two years later when I sent out a newsletter saying that we were hiring director-level positions. When we met in person, I lost my shit. I couldn't hear anything he said, which had never happened to me before—love at first sight. When I tried to interview him over tea, I realized I couldn't hire him because I couldn't even focus enough to read his resume. After I confessed this, he took the resumes off the table and asked if I'd go to dinner with him instead. Derek never had vegan friends before, let alone a vegan girlfriend, so he was all sorts of crazy excited about all the benefits—that we get to make food together, split meals at restaurants, and we have an ongoing list of all the places we want to eat at together. Our shared connection makes everyday things more fun and easy—like exploring neighborhoods and new cities together. But veganism is also a sign of basic things like self-awareness, discipline, a proactive personality, and compassion that I find super sexy and a requirement in a partner.

"My top tip for vegans looking for love is that if you're looking for someone, omni or vegan, look for someone who has the same reasons for being vegan. Are you vegan because you're compassionate and self-aware? Then focus on looking for those features while dating. You can find a vegan who's negative and self-focused. Just because they're vegan doesn't mean they're a good match for you."

Habanero Jackfruit Fajitas

Prep time: 10 minutes | Cook time: 30 minutes | Serves 2 to 4 | GF

The first time I had jackfruit was in LA. About ten years ago, my friend Saul Williams took me to a place, now closed, that served jackfruit barbeque hoagies. He told me they taste just like pulled pork. Of course, I've never tried pulled pork, but nowadays I see jackfruit pulled pork sandwiches everywhere. I like the texture of the fruit, and in this recipe, I amped up the flavor by adding one of my favorite ingredients: chile peppers. Adding a bit of habanero hot sauce in addition to the fresh habanero enhances that peppery goodness without calling for an entire bushel of chiles. You can experiment with extra habaneros, with or without seeds, finely minced. But I warn you: use at your own risk. Enjoy!

JACKFRUIT

2 tablespoons grapeseed or safflower oil

1 (20-ounce) can jackfruit (packed in water or
    brine, *not* sugar), drained

2 tablespoons chopped fresh sage

1/2 teaspoon habanero hot sauce

2 tablespoons nutritional yeast

2 tablespoons vegan Worcestershire sauce

2 tablespoons low-sodium wheat-free tamari

1 tablespoon brown sugar

1/2 teaspoon habanero hot sauce

Salt

1 cup water

1 (12-ounce) package 10-inch flour or corn tortillas

FAJITAS

2 tablespoons grapeseed or safflower oil

1/2 cup sliced onion

1/2 green bell pepper, sliced lengthwise

1/2 yellow bell pepper, sliced lengthwise

1/2 red bell pepper, sliced lengthwise

Salt

Vegan sour cream (optional)

Lemon or lime wedges (optional)

1. Jackfruit: Heat the oil in a medium skillet over medium-high heat. Add the jackfruit and break it into shreds with a fork. Add the sage and minced habanero. Add the nutritional yeast, Worcestershire sauce, tamari, brown sugar, and hot sauce. Add salt to taste and stir in the water to incorporate well. Cover and simmer for 30 minutes on low heat. Taste and adjust salt and spice to your liking. Remove from the heat. Preheat the oven to 350°F.

2. While the jackfruit braises, wrap the tortillas in foil and place in the preheated oven for 10 minutes.

3. Fajitas: Heat the oil in a medium skillet over medium-high heat. Add the onion and bell peppers, and sprinkle with salt to taste. Sauté until the vegetables begin to caramelize, 8 to 10 minutes. Remove from the heat and transfer to a serving bowl.

4. Set up a family-style serving station with the warm tortillas, peppers and onions, jackfruit, and optional vegan sour cream with lemon wedges, extra hot sauce, chips, cheese shreds…you get the idea.

5 THINGS YOU DIDN'T KNOW ABOUT JACKFRUIT

Most of us probably don't know jack about jackfruit. (See what we did there?) The fruit is pretty obscure compared to more popular tropical fruits like pineapple and papaya. Let's change that.

1. Jackfruit is actually part of the mulberry family, although it looks nothing like a mulberry.

2. It can be eaten raw or cooked. In the U.S, it is most readily found canned, although you can probably rustle up a fresh fruit at an Asian supermarket.

3. Jackfruit is high in potassium, which makes it a good post-workout grab.

4. The seeds are high in protein. If you can get your hands on a freshie, add the seeds to your favorite dishes for an extra protein punch.

5. Jackfruit is high in copper, which plays an important role in hormone production and maintaining a healthy metabolism.

Cauliflower Steak
with Miso-Rooster Sauce

Prep time: 30 minutes | Cook time: 8 minutes | Serves 2 | GF, SF

In exploring the plant world, it's nice to come across a plant with a natural texture that is good enough to eat on its own. With this recipe, I wanted to combine textures and flavors: the soft, almost creamy texture of cooked cauliflower, the deep, pungent flavor of the fermented miso, and the spicy kick of sriracha, or as I call it, rooster sauce. I created this dish for one of my private clients, and it quickly became a menu staple. I think it will be on yours as well.

CAULIFLOWER

2 tablespoon grapeseed or safflower oil

2 cauliflower steaks (see Pro-Tip)

1/2 cup leeks, white and light green
    parts only, cut in wheels

1 tablespoon nutritional yeast

2 teaspoons minced fresh oregano

1 teaspoon smoked paprika

1/2 teaspoon red pepper flakes

1/2 teaspoon sea salt

SAUCE

1 tablespoon vegan butter

1/2 cup onion, diced

1 teaspoon minced garlic

1 teaspoon minced fresh ginger

3/4 cup water

1 tablespoon chickpea miso

1 tablespoon sriracha

1 teaspoon cornstarch

1 teaspoon toasted sesame seed oil

1/4 teaspoon sea salt

2 fresh thyme sprigs, for garnish

1. Cauliflower: Preheat the oven to 250°F. Heat the oil in a medium oven-safe skillet over medium-high heat until hot and shimmering. Place the cauliflower steaks and leeks in the hot skillet and cook for approximately 3 minutes on each side. Working quickly, sprinkle the nutritional yeast, oregano, paprika, red pepper flakes, and salt evenly on both sides. Transfer the skillet to the oven to keep warm. Turn off the oven and keep it closed.

2. Sauce: In a medium skillet over medium heat, heat the butter until hot. Add the onions and sauté until caramelized, approximately 6 minutes. Add the garlic and ginger and sauté for additional 2 to 3 minutes.

3. In a measuring cup, combine the water with the miso, sriracha, cornstarch, sesame oil, and salt. Whisk thoroughly to combine. Add the liquid mixture to the skillet with the onion mixture and mix well with a whisk. Once the sauce begins to thicken, reduce the heat to low. To adjust the flavor of the sauce, simply add more water by the tablespoon until it is to your taste.

4. Plating: Place a cauliflower steak in the center of each plate, followed by a spoonful of the leeks. Drizzle the warm sauce over and around the cauliflower and garnish with a sprig of fresh thyme. Serve hot.

Pro-Tip: How to Carve Cauliflower Steaks: Knife skill time, guys! Place a head of cauliflower on a cutting board. Make a slightly off-center cut down the middle of the cauliflower. You now have two halves; one will be slightly bigger. Take the bigger half and cut two 1-inch thick steaks from it.

7. ENTER THE VEG

Fried Tofu Sandwich, page 161

"Tofu: the missionary position of the vegan world."

Calling the omnivore...good, you are still reading, so you must be in! You're into your vegan, and you may be eating less meat yourself. No? Okay, well you at least want to try cooking less meat, even if you're just trying to use your cooking skills as a means of wooing. Well woo, woo, woo as they say.

AYINDÉ: Ginger would occasionally buy tofu and try to do something with it. After she made her experimental dinner, the other half of the white gelatinous block would sit there until the bacteria began to have a party, and then it would inevitably be thrown out. Most people just don't know what to do with it. But worry not, for I will teach you. I hate to see good tofu go to waste. I wanted to create recipes that either use the whole block or halves and quarters, since that's what's left after the scramble you made that was just okay.

Personally, I love tofu. I really grew up on it and do love it. Knowing your tofu, and getting over any fear you have of it, will help you impress your new vegan. Let's spend a little time talking about it before we get into cooking it.

The low-down on tofu

The first question I always hear from men is "Will it give you man boobs?" I have eaten tofu all my life, and I have no man boobs.

The second question, from women, is "Will it give me breast cancer?" According to cancer.org, research has shown that soy in moderate consumption is safe for both breast cancer survivors and the general population. Some studies even say that soy may prevent breast cancer. But as usual, moderation is key, so use tofu and almond milk so there's no soy-on-soy action.

That being said, you still have to look out for the good, the bad, and the cheap.

The Good: Organic, non-GMO tofu (or tempeh) with organic soybeans as the main ingredient.

The Bad: Soy protein isolate. This is the protein of soy extracted to make cheap protein filler in everything from processed meat to crackers. Read labels; it's in just about everything.

The Cheap: Non-organic tofu in unidentifiable packaging. Look for a trusted brand. I have been eating Island Spring tofu since I was a kid. There are other good brands out there, so do your research.

I also often use tempeh with my clients. Unlike tofu, tempeh is fermented and thus easier on the digestive tract of those with common digestive issues. Personally, I prefer tofu.

So real the key here is to watch your soy intake by paying attention to the fillers in processed foods. Start by eliminating as many processed foods as possible, and be aware that when you get that fake chicken sandwich, it's probably the cheap kind of soy.

Now that you have the lowdown on tofu, you can start cooking with it! Say with confidence: "Yes, I can enjoy this versatile, cholesterol-free food in a way that is delicious and nutritious, and I can finally understand why it's the cornerstone of veganism!" That sounded quite presidential, or should I say kingly? Welcome to vegan land!

FIVE THINGS TO KNOW FOR COOKING WITH TOFU

Here are five fun facts I have come up with for taming this white beast.

1. Read the label. If it doesn't say organic and non-GMO, put it back!

2. You can freeze tofu to change the consistency completely. I do this if I want a chewier texture. Just pop the whole package in the freezer, then thaw it out and use as normal.

3. There are different kinds for a reason: silken, soft, firm, and extra-firm. Pick a form that will be best for what you're making. A firmer variety is great for grilling, and a softer version is best for scrambles.

4. Use your leftover tofu as an accent. You can always brown some tofu in a skillet and add it to something, like soup, stir fry, salad, or chili. There's always room for tofu.

5. Tofu is a blank protein canvas. Instead of seeing it as bland, you should see possibilities when you look at it. It soaks up any flavor you throw at it.

ZOË: Many consider "tofu" and "vegan" synonymous. Unfortunately, many also consider "tofu" synonymous with "bland," "boring," and "texturally challenged." Okay, I made that last one up, but you get what I mean. Tofu, done right, is fucking delicious. But when done wrong—and many, many people do it wrong—it can be a bit of a bummer in terms of both texture and flavor.

Maybe you and tofu have a complicated history. You had one bad experience plated up years ago by a macrobiotic aunt, and now the only tofu you want to eat is no tofu. Sure, you can enjoy it fried, because you could deep-fry a geometry textbook and it would probably still be delicious, but you're better than that, right? Right! Whether it's seared, sautéed, roasted, grilled, or scrambled, after you've gone through the recipes in this chapter, you'll be a tofu pro. But before that, let's get back to me and Danny boy for a hot second.

Daniel and I were living together. We were speaking in the first-person plural. We shared a cat (whom I appropriately named Zucchini), but even more importantly, we shared a Netflix queue. I suspect my parents were furiously stashing money away for a wedding with fingers crossed and breath held. Because we were happy and young and in love—a trifecta that often ends in dumb decision-making—the M word was actually being tossed around.

Ah, love. Daniel and I had gone from drunkenly petting one another, to dating casually, to dating exclusively, to family bonding, to living together. During that four-year period, Daniel's diet started to change. It wasn't radical, and it wasn't planned, but it did happen. By the time cohabitation came around, he was choosing meat-free options when we dined out. He was also choosing all meat-free options at the grocery store, without any input from me. There were often ulterior motives for this. Meat tended to be the more expensive choice, and we were pretty broke.

I didn't want to comment too much on the changes I noticed in Daniel's eating habits, or get any kind of "maybe he will go veg!" hope only to watch it smashed on the rocks of meaty disappointment. I just hung back and let him do his thing and hoped he didn't notice me lurking behind him at the grocery store, cackling to myself over his selection of dairy-free chocolate bars.

Daniel was proving to be a great partner. He was kind and thoughtful, but most importantly, he liked tofu. Or at least, it seemed like he did. He frequently ordered it from our favorite Thai restaurant, and happily scarfed down my signature sweet ginger tofu dish, which we called "Sexy Tofu." Actually, Daniel liked most of the things I put on his plate. After several years of enthusiastic responses to even the most experimental of my culinary creations, I realized that his enthusiasm probably had nothing to do with my cooking or an affection for tofu. The reality most likely was that Daniel just liked me. That was cool, too.

Stories from the Field

Jules Febre, Jivamukti Yoga teacher

"Since, for me, veganism is not a choice of taste but comes from a moral way of being, it can make relationships very easy, or less easy. I would prefer to share the desire to cause less harm with my partner. Having a level of comfort with the one you are being intimate with, so that you feel good about what they put in their body and how that comes from a large heart, makes it special. There are more vegans than non-vegans at the moment, so perhaps the field of possible romance is diminished, but when it works, it really works well.

My top tip for vegans looking for love is to let love, the desire to receive it and the desire to give it, be what guides your choice. Only you can really decide what is right and what you want."

"Enter the Veg"

An intro to tofu

"*If you're going out to eat, understand that most good chefs enjoy a challenge: you can go to a nice restaurant with your omni partner and request a meal that fits your needs. I've been pleasantly surprised many times doing this.*" – DREW, VEGAN

Classic Tofu Loaf

Prep time: 15 minutes | Cook time: 40 minutes | Serves 4 to 6 | GFO

This meal is perfect for those times you open up the fridge and the selection looks sparse. All you've got is a package of tofu and an abundance of condiments. The recipe may seem simple, but that's exactly why it's here. Every now and then you have to hit the easy button, and for a simple staple like this, you shouldn't try and over-think it. If you have a package of tofu and you don't want it to go bad, this will solve that problem and give you leftovers. You can mix and match with sides. It pairs well with the savory bread pudding on page 114 or the pickled fennel salad on page 99. Use gluten-free oats to make this gluten-free.

1 tablespoon grapeseed or safflower oil

14 ounces firm tofu, well-drained

1 1/2 cups old-fashioned rolled oats

1/2 cup chopped flat-leaf parsley

1/2 cup chopped onion

1 teaspoon minced garlic

1/2 cup ketchup

1/4 cup Dijon mustard

1/4 cup barbecue sauce

1/4 cup low-sodium wheat-free tamari

1/2 teaspoon salt

For garnish: ketchup; chopped fresh parsley

1. Preheat the oven to 350°F. Grease a 9x5-inch loaf pan with the oil and set aside.

2. In a large mixing bowl, crumble the tofu into bite-size pieces. Add the oats and mix well. Stir in the parsley, onion, and garlic. Add the ketchup, mustard, barbecue sauce, tamari, and salt. Mix well, until all ingredients are incorporated.

3. Press the mixture evenly into the prepared pan. Bake for 30 minutes.

4. Serve garnished with ketchup and fresh parsley.

Pro-tip: Try cooking this recipe in muffin cups for individual serving sizes, ideal for brown-bagging your lunches during the work week.

Tofu Ricotta Crostini

Prep time: 5 minutes | Serves 2 to 4 | GFO

I came up with this recipe during Ginger's experimental tofu period. She would leave opened blocks laying in the fridge, and I was tired of watching them go bad. Late one night, I wanted to make a quick snack, and stumbled upon one of her half-eaten tofu packages. I put together this ricotta and slathered it on some crispy vegan buttered whole grain toast. It makes a great protein-filled snack and allows you to use up that half-block of tofu lying in your fridge. Use gluten-free bread to make this gluten-free.

8 ounces firm tofu, drained well and
    patted with paper towels

1 tablespoon + 1 teaspoon finely
    chopped fresh basil

1 tablespoon capers

1 teaspoon dried oregano

1 teaspoon nutritional yeast

1 1/2 teaspoons salt

1 tablespoon grapeseed or safflower oil

1 tablespoon minced garlic

1 1/2 teaspoons fresh lemon juice

2 slices bread, any kind

1 teaspoon nutritional yeast

1. In a medium bowl, break up the tofu with a fork until it is the consistency of ricotta cheese. Add the basil, capers, oregano, nutritional yeast, and salt. Mix well.

2. In a medium skillet over medium-high heat, heat the oil until hot. Add the garlic and sauté until golden, about 30 seconds. dd the tofu mixture and sauté for 3 to 5 minutes, or until hot. Stir in the lemon juice.

3. Toast 2 slices of bread and cut each one into 4 triangles. Slather on the ricotta and serve.

Paella

Prep time: 5 minutes | Cook time: 35 minutes | Serves 4 | GF

Paella is a traditional Spanish seafood dish typically prepared and presented in a huge pan, unoriginally called a paella pan. As we've addressed already, tofu can be substituted for just about any animal protein, so tofu paella is a tasty spin on the original. The hearts of palm act as a replacement for crab-meat and the laundry list of herbs and spices are what attracted me—a reality cooking show host once told me that I like my food powerfully seasoned. Ha, you're damn right! Olé!

2 tablespoons grapeseed or safflower oil

1 tablespoon vegan butter

8 ounces firm tofu, cut into bite-sized pieces

1 (14-ounce) can hearts of palm, drained and torn into shreds

2 cups water

1/2 cup chopped red bell pepper

1/2 cup, chopped green bell pepper

1/2 cup chopped celery

1/2 cup chopped onion

1 tablespoon minced garlic

1 tablespoon chopped fresh rosemary

1 tablespoon Old Bay seasoning

10 threads of saffron

2 teaspoons smoked paprika

1 teaspoon dried basil

1 1/2 cups dry brown basmati rice

2 cups water

1 teaspoons salt

2 cups cored, seeded, and chopped plum tomatoes

2 teaspoons salt

Freshly cracked black pepper

1. Heat the oil and butter in a large skillet over medium-high heat. Add the tofu and sauté until it reaches a crisp texture and golden-brown color, approximately 5 to 7 minutes. Stir occasionally with a spatula to prevent burning.

2. Add the hearts of palm and sauté for additional 3 minutes, until browned.

3. Add the bell peppers, celery, onion, and garlic, and sauté over medium heat for 5 minutes, stirring occasionally. Add the rosemary, Old Bay seasoning, saffron, smoked paprika, and basil. Add the rice and slowly pour in the water and salt.

4. Stir in the tomatoes and reduce the heat to medium-low. Cover and cook until the rice has absorbed the water, approximately 35 minutes, or until it reaches a nutty, al dente texture. Remove from the heat and season with salt and pepper to taste. Serve hot.

5 Things You Didn't Know About Hearts of Palm

This is the third time you've seen hearts of palm starring in a recipe in this book, so you're probably wondering what this veggie is all about. Here are a few informational nuggets about this beloved vegetable.

1. Heart of palm is also known as chonta, palm cabbage, or—my favorite—swamp cabbage.

2. It is harvested from the growing bud of a palm tree, thus the name.

3. Move over, bananas. Heart of palm is chock full of potassium, as well as vitamin C, zinc, and phosphorous.

4. Heart of palm is super-high in iron, providing 25 percent RDI per serving.

5. The chewy texture and mild sweetness naturally found in the palm heart makes it a great plant-based substitute for fish.

Fried Tofu Sandwich

Prep time: 25 minutes | Cook time: 10 minutes | Serves 2 | GFO

What would this book be without a romantic comedy? Ever seen the movie Spanglish with Adam Sandler? There is a scene before he discovers his wife is cheating on him (spoiler alert) and he has a moment of peace. He does what most chefs do: he makes a [fried egg] sandwich for himself and is about to eat it when hijinks ensue. Anyway, this is my version of a fried egg sandwich. In every love, romance, and break-up, there is always food, right? Use gluten-free bread to make this gluten-free.

QUICK PICKLED CUCUMBERS

1/2 cup sliced English cucumber

1/2 teaspoon salt

1/2 teaspoon cracked black pepper

1 tablespoon white balsamic vinegar

TOFU

1/4 cup water

2 tablespoons low-sodium wheat-free tamari

1 teaspoon chopped fresh sage

1 teaspoon nutritional yeast

1 teaspoon chopped garlic

1/2 teaspoon chopped fresh thyme

1/2 teaspoon chili powder

1/4 teaspoon white pepper

1/4 teaspoon liquid smoke

2 tablespoons grapeseed or safflower oil

8 ounces extra-firm tofu, frozen and thawed and cut lengthwise into 3-inch long slices, 1/8 inch thick

ASSEMBLY

4 slices sourdough bread

Mustard

Cucumber chips

Optional toppings: hot sauce, grilled onions, sliced Beefsteak tomatoes, winter salad mix

1. Cucumbers: Place the cucumber chips on a plate and sprinkle salt and pepper on both sides. Pour balsamic vinegar on top and set aside for 5 to 10 minutes.

2. Tofu: In a shallow bowl, combine the water, tamari, sage, nutritional yeast, garlic, thyme, chili powder, white pepper, and liquid smoke, and set aside. Add the sliced tofu to the bowl and marinate for 20 minutes.

3. Heat the oil in a skillet over medium-high heat. Add the tofu and pan-fry until golden brown on both sides, approximately 6 minutes total. Add the marinade to the pan. Cover and cook on medium-low until the marinade evaporates, approximately 8 minutes.

4. Assembly: Toast the bread to desired crispness. Spread a thin layer of mustard onto the bread, and arrange two slices of the tofu on top of two of the bread slices. Top the tofu with a few cucumber chips and other toppings of your choice, then place the remaining slices of bread on top.

Mexican Lasagna

Prep time: 10 minutes | Cook time: 45 minutes | Serves 4 to 6 | GF

After I quit my executive chef position in New York City, I started doing private catering. My very first gig was actually for a friend of a friend, and they hired me to cook for a party. At the time, I didn't know I was expected to clean up after catering events, because I was a chef and was used to people cleaning up after me. I made this lasagna, which was a hit with everyone; I bowed and said thank you, and they then asked me to clean up. I looked at them like "Whaaaat?" All in all, this lasagna is great and unexpected, much like my clean-up gig. This is another great "eat for the week" meal that can be cut into portions for freezing and reheating later.

1/4 cup grapeseed or safflower oil

8 ounces firm tofu, drained and crumbled

1 cup chopped red onion, divided

4 tablespoons Mexican Spice Blend, divided (page 215)

1/4 cup water

2 tablespoons low-sodium wheat-free tamari

1 teaspoon salt

2 cups medium salsa, divided

1 package (5-inch) corn tortillas

1 cup shredded vegan mozzarella cheese

1 cup shredded vegan cheddar cheese

1 cup sliced mushrooms

3/4 cup corn kernels, fresh or frozen

1/2 cup chopped green bell pepper

2 tablespoons nutritional yeast

3/4 cup canned black beans

1. Heat the oil in a medium skillet over medium-high heat until hot. Add the tofu and sauté, stirring frequently, until golden brown and crispy, 7 to 10 minutes.

2. Add 1/4 cup red onion and sauté for 4 minutes. Add 2 tablespoons Mexican spice blend and mix well. Add the water, soy sauce, and salt. Reduce the heat to low, cover, and simmer until all the spices have incorporated into the tofu, approximately 3 minutes. Remove from the heat and set aside. Preheat the oven to 375°F.

3. Pour 3/4 cup salsa in the bottom of a lightly-oiled 8-inch square baking dish. Cover the salsa with 2 to 3 corn tortillas. Layer all the tofu mixture on top of the tortillas. Top with half of the mozzarella cheese, cheddar cheese, mushrooms, corn, bell pepper, remaining red onion, and 1/2 cup of the salsa. Sprinkle with 1 tablespoon of the nutritional yeast. Place 2 to 3 tortillas on top to cover. Top with a layer of black beans and sprinkle on 1 tablespoon of Mexican spice blend. Layer on the remaining cheese, mushrooms, corn, bell pepper, and red onion.

4. Pour the remaining 3/4 cup salsa on top, layer more tortillas on top and rub with oil, covering the entire surface of the tortillas. Top with the remaining 1 tablespoon of the spice blend and 1 tablespoon nutritional yeast. Cover with foil and bake for 45 minutes. Remove the foil after 45 minutes and bake uncovered for 5 to 7 minutes longer, just until tortillas are crisp on top.

Blasian Fried Rice

Prep time: 8 minutes | Cook time: 10 minutes | Serves 2 to 4 | GF

Fried rice is a dish I always love. I asked myself, why go out and order it, when you can make at home? And because I believe that all black people put their spin on Asian food when they make it at home—or at least I do—I call this one Blasian (Black Asian) Fried Rice, homestyle cooking headed east. Despite the spin, it still has the familiar fried rice flavors that you can find in your local take-out place.

2 tablespoons grapeseed or safflower oil

1/2 teaspoon toasted sesame oil

1/4 pound firm tofu, drained and cut into triangles 1/8 inch thick

1 1/2 cups sliced leeks, cut into wheels

1/2 cup chopped onion

1/2 cup chopped bell pepper

1/4 cup chopped celery

2 teaspoons chopped fresh garlic

1/2 cup corn kernels

2 cups cooked basmati rice

2 tablespoons low-sodium wheat-free tamari

1 tablespoon hoisin sauce

1 teaspoon nutritional yeast

1 teaspoon salt

1. Heat both oils in a medium skillet over medium-high heat until hot. Add the tofu and cook until brown on all sides, turning once, about 5 minutes total. Tofu will absorb the oil, so feel free to add more. I trust you. Once the tofu is done, remove it from the oil, leaving the skillet on the heat.

2. To the hot skillet, add the leeks, onion, bell pepper, celery, and garlic and cook until the onion becomes translucent, 3 to 5 minutes.

3. Add the corn and sauté for 2 minutes, then stir in the rice, tamari, hoisin sauce, nutritional yeast, and salt, stirring well until all ingredients are incorporated. Add the tofu back into the skillet. Cook for about 5 minutes on medium-low heat. Serve hot.

Lemon Pepper Poppers

Prep time: 35 minutes | Cook time 10 minutes | Serves 2 to 4 | GF

It was brought to my attention that I had no recipes for what we call these days "ratchet." Ratchet means ghetto fab—think Red Lobster and Olive Garden types of food. The point was made that even though people want to eat healthy, they still want old favorites. And since lemon pepper is a spice all people own and a favorite amongst the ratchet set, I thought I'd deconstruct it and make it healthy! The marinade uses lemon pepper seasoning to add flavor and the eggy chickpea batter adds a light, crunchy coating. These are great for dipping in your favorite sauces and a healthy snack for kids and ratchets alike.

TOFU AND ZUCCHINI

12 ounces extra-firm tofu, drained and
    cut in 1-inch slices

1/2 cup lemon juice

2 tablespoons granulated sugar

1 teaspoon lemon zest

1 teaspoon garlic powder

1 teaspoon onion powder

1/2 teaspoon freshly ground black pepper

1 cup diced zucchini

BATTER

1/2 cup chickpea flour

1/4 cup nutritional yeast

1 teaspoon lemon pepper seasoning

1 teaspoon sea salt

1/2 teaspoon fresh black pepper

1/2 cup water

1/4 cup grapeseed or safflower oil (for
    cooking)

1. Press the tofu slices for about 10 minutes to remove the excess water, then cut the tofu into 1-inch cubes. In a shallow bowl, combine the lemon juice, sugar, lemon zest, garlic powder, onion powder, and black pepper. Add the tofu and zucchini and set aside for 25 minutes to marinate, stirring occasionally.

2. In a mixing bowl, combine the chickpea flour, nutritional yeast, lemon pepper seasoning, salt, and black pepper. While whisking, slowly add the water until it reaches pancake batter consistency.

3. Add tofu, zucchini, and marinade to the batter, stirring to coat completely. Set aside until you are ready to fry.

4. Heat the oil in a medium skillet over medium-high heat until hot. Add the pieces of battered tofu and zucchini to the hot oil, cooking on all sides until golden brown, approximately 5 minutes total. Once done, place in a paper-towel-lined bowl to drain excess oil. Serve hot with choice of dips. I like BBQ sauce and sriracha.

Thai Tofu Scramble

Prep time: 5 minutes | Cook time: 10 minutes | Serves 2 | GF

I wanted to try a tofu scramble in a different way -- something with a kick. I treated it like dinner and it turned out amazing, but this spicy scramble is best made with the oven fan on. Cooking with hot chiles creates fumes that can burn your eyes or make you cough. To avoid this in poorly-ventilated spaces, omit the Thai chiles from the recipe and add extra sriracha after it's done.

2 tablespoons grapeseed or safflower oil

8 ounces firm tofu, drained

2 tablespoons chopped onion

1 teaspoon grated ginger

1 teaspoon minced Thai basil

1 tablespoon hoisin sauce

1 teaspoon toasted sesame seed oil

1 teaspoon dry white wine

1/2 teaspoon chili paste or sriracha

1 Thai chile, seeded and minced

1. Heat the oil in a medium skillet over medium-high heat until hot and shimmering. Using your hands, crumble the tofu into the skillet. Sauté for 2 to 4 minutes, stirring occasionally.

2. Add the onion, ginger, and Thai basil. Sauté until the onion becomes translucent, then reduce the heat to medium.

3. In a small bowl, whisk together the hoisin sauce, sesame oil, wine, and chili paste or Sriracha. Add to the skillet and cook until the liquid evaporates, 1 to 2 minutes. Remove from the heat and stir in the minced chile.

Stories from the Field

Hannah Kaminsky, author of *Easy as Vegan Pie*

"Being vegan is definitely a defining aspect of my life, and that narrows down the field considerably and ensures that you wind up with someone compassionate enough to at least respect your lifestyle decisions. A relationship is a two-way street, so the least that I can do in return is accept an omnivorous partner's eating and purchasing preferences as they do mine. That's not to say that I wouldn't engage them in a conversation about it, but I wouldn't let it completely color my opinion of someone, nor would I find a response that I don't agree with an indication of incompatibility. Also, people change over time, especially with repeated exposure, even without a conscious effort. Even if you start out dating an omnivore, they may not always stay that way."

"Excuse me, I need to go eat my feelings."

Living together does many things for a couple, and one of them is showing you how you function—or don't function—as a single entity. One big breathing-eating-laughing-f*cking-fighting-crying machine. Cohabitation shines a big bright spotlight on your flaws, your incompatibilities, and how much work needs to be done as a pair if you want to continue on your journey into The Future.

ZOË: They say it's the little things that matter when you're falling in love. They don't tell you it's the little things that matter when you're falling out, too. "They" are kind of idealistic assholes, whoever they are.

It was a little thing that woke me up to the fact Daniel and I weren't going to make it. Actually, it wasn't a thing, it was a thought. A thought that popped into my mind one night over dinner. A thought so completely irrational, I actually glanced over both shoulders to see what total lunatic just opened their mouth, because it couldn't possibly have come out of my own brain.

You see, I cared about Daniel a lot. I knew what a good guy he was, but when it came to our connection, something was just off. It wasn't the lifestyle differences, although that added to it. There were certain aspects of our personalities that just didn't align.

Growing up in suburban Connecticut, I was the weird kid. You know, the one whose presence was always punctuated with a conspiratory "Who invited her?" eye-roll passed between my peers. It could have been the macrobiotic food I brought for lunch (thanks, Ma!) or the fact that my knees were double-jointed and everyone called me "banana legs." I had no filter and often spoke my thoughts, which were received with a chorus of blank stares. As a result, I spent the majority of my adolescence feeling like no one "got" me.

Where am I going with this? Well, during my relationship with Dan, there were some big moments that reminded me what it felt like to be the only fifth grader not invited to Susie P's pool party. I often felt like he didn't really understand me. I can't blame him, really. After twenty-six years with myself, I know that I'm an acquired taste. But when I imagined my life in five, ten, fifteen years, I just couldn't see us together.

And that's where my looney tunes moment came in. At the time, Daniel was waiting tables at a nearby pub while he figured out his grad school situation. (Not one vegan thing on the menu there, by the way.)

One night before his shift at work—oh, he wore the cutest little apron—Dan mentioned casually that a new hostess had started that day. My immediate

thought, while lifting a forkful of caramelized asparagus to my mouth, was "Good; I hope you cheat on me so I can dump you without feeling guilty." Um, what? Go home, brain, you're drunk.

I was scared of hurting Dan, and so I had irrationally begun to look for justifications that would sting less than the truth, which was: "I'm not in love with you anymore."

IF IT'S NOT A YES, IT'S A NO.

You see, up until that point, I had never been the villain in a relationship. Before Dan, whenever I broke up with someone, it was because they cheated, or lied, or lit my car on fire in a fit of jealous rage.

If I've learned one thing from my relationships, it's that I really do prefer bottom over top. No, not that; it's this: if given the choice, I'd rather get pain than give pain. Being hurt is rotten, but when it's you who is doing the damage, you're dealt something worse than heartbreak: guilt. Oh man, the guilt. I'd rather have a bruised ego than a plate full of guilt, any day.

But a fear of your own impending evil isn't enough of a reason to stay with someone, and so after over three years of dating and six months of cohabitation, I packed up my juicer, my blender, AND my food processor drove the eight hours back to my parent's house in Connecticut.

The end. Sort of.

While the relationship didn't work, I like to focus on the positive. We had fun, and we managed to get into a pretty good groove with the vegan/omni food situation. So good, in fact, that when I left, Daniel actually asked if he could keep a few of my vegan cookbooks now that he was fending for himself. "Fine! But not my favorites. Don't you even think about asking for any of my Isa Chandra Moskowitz! Step AWAY from *Vegan Brunch*."

It was exactly one week post-split that I received an interesting text from Daniel. After reading a copy of Jonathan Safran Foer's *Eating Animals* that I had left behind, he had decided to stop eating meat. Really, Universe? Really? What kind of backass karma is that?

AYINDÉ: By late winter 2011, Ginger and I were growing apart. Our differences were becoming too big to cover up with great sex. I had quit my executive chef job at that Union Square restaurant, and got into a work-study program to finish acting school. I started doing pop-up restaurants around town. I moved off our subway line. Now, in Brooklyn, living off different subway lines is like living in two different states. You have to take a train, and a bus, if you're lucky.

My lease was up and Ginger wanted to live together, and I didn't. I had shacked up once before in the early 2000s and it was no bueno. Ginger had not lived with anyone and thought it was a splendid idea, and was upset that I moved to the "hood" part of Brooklyn and not in with her.

As an adult, I had never been so involved with a woman. Aside from food politics, everything else worked really well, save one or two major things. So I was panicked and stalling, trying to figure out if this was how it was supposed to feel. Is it really 80/20? You know the theory: 80 percent of exactly what you want vs. 20 percent of what you don't. It's that grown-up stuff nobody tells you about, like how is it supposed to feel right before you say, "Eff it, I'm gonna put my faith in this one"—then, jump. Are you still scared? Or is fear the red flag?

It was clear that she was never going to be a vegan, though in the end, that wasn't the last straw. If I'm honest with myself today, I'd say it was a colossal power struggle, an exercise in non-compromise. It was seeing the real person and deciding how you actually fit together: flaws, crazy shit, and all. One sees "Get out while you can," and the other sees "You have no faith in me." You're both right.

My truth is different today. So today I'd say before you get too far into it, just stand back and ask yourself: could you be with this person as they are today, ten, twenty, fifty years from now, if they NEVER change? If the answer is not yes, then it's a no. So, you should wait not for perfection, but for the right balance of the 80/20. When the 80 percent of what you want is standing in front of you, don't focus on trying to change the 20 percent, because that part may never change, and maybe it shouldn't. Of course, hindsight is 20/20.

We ultimately broke up because of a power struggle, with both of us having too much pride to compromise on a couple of really huge things. It was a hard lesson learned. After a few drunken calls and sex interrupted by crying, it was over. The last time I saw her, I helped her move...to LA. She went without me. She went ahead with her plans and, like in any good rom-com, I was supposed to either stop her or come with her. I did neither. I was just a good friend and helped her move her entire life prematurely, neither of us willing to compromise in the last moments. I said goodbye and took a bus to a train back home. The next day I had to either accept it or throw myself into work. So, during the coping phase of the break-up, I did more pop-up restaurants. My catering business, Wildflower, was born. I did reality TV and ate a lot of sweets. Pie was my needle of choice. I gained a few pounds in those days. Gradually, I began to get back in my solo mode. I did this while slipping back into the loving arms of my true love: sugar. Because sometimes you just want a pan of cinnamon rolls! I deserve one, or else somebody's getting cried on.

How to survive a sucky breakup (Isn't every breakup a sucky breakup?)

ZOË: Breakups blow, and not in the good way. Unlike Ayindé, I'm not much of a breakup eater. I am, however, a break-up social binger. I'm also slightly embarrassed to admit I'm a weeper. I've cried hard over splits with people I didn't even like much to begin with.

Crying aside, my immediate breakup coping mechanism is to surround myself with people. After the split with Daniel, I lost my mind for a bit. Having relocated back to the East Coast where I grew up, I reconnected with my old drinking crowd and spent a couple of seasons out late and up early. It felt like college all over again, but with a valid ID, no dorm rooms, and work the next day. I tagged along with friends to bars and venues I really had no interest in visiting, not in hopes of meeting new potential sexy time candidates (remember, no more picking up singles at karaoke...), but because I just didn't want to be alone during that first stretch. I was that girl. When I found myself alone, I would be tempted to call Daniel out of habit, which wasn't good for either of us.

I would also mope, and mope hard. While I knew I shouldn't be with Daniel, and I wasn't ready for a new relationship, I wanted someone to cuddle and cook for. I was lonely, and I was trying to evade this loneliness by keeping extremely busy. This tactic doesn't work in the long run, because no matter how busy you make yourself, the moping is inevitable—that solo car ride to work will always find you.

Here are a few tips for getting by after a breakup. I will avoid the overly obvious, like no stalking or revenge-boning their roommates...

1. Allow yourself to be somewhat miserable for awhile. "Fake it till you make it" doesn't work with breakups. If you ignore your emotions, you will shower your next partner with a slew of projectile feelings that really had nothing to do with them in the first place. Allow yourself to have a good cry or several good cries. Make yourself an extra emo breakup playlist and spend a few hours with it on repeat. But then get your shit together, man! Don't cry in the bathroom at work. Don't cry in the cubicle at work. Don't text your coworker and say, "Omggg, I just broke up with my boyfriend, please bring me a soy latté!" Because breaking up sucks, but so does getting fired for being a mess. Messes are not professional.

2. But keep an eye on the emo parade. I am the queen of nostalgic sadism. I often do my best (read: most emotionally gut-wrenching) writing when I'm miserable, so I tend to puddle for too long. I think it took me seven years to fully get over my high school sweet-heart, not because I still had feelings for him, but because being dejected makes me feel dramatic and complex. Don't do this. It is not healthy. Don't pore through photos or memen-tos and make yourself more miserable. You know that breakup playlist? After a few weeks of listening to it on repeat, throw it out. Do it. Out the window. Okay, well, no littering, but at least in the trash. Get your good cries out, have a few pity parties, eat a couple (dozen) cookies—looking at you, Ayindé—and then pull it together.

3. Try not to do anything that will make you feel bad about yourself. After a breakup, you probably already feel bad, so don't make it worse. Remember the dozen cookies? If those cookies are going to make you hate yourself tomorrow, then try to abstain. Avoid whatever it is that triggers a guilt hangover. For some, it's emotional eating. For others, it's too-soon, too-casual sex, or taking out your frustration on people who are just trying to be nice. Avoid things that will make me generally ashamed of myself. I mean, YOU of yourself. We are taking about you. Not me.

4. Keep social media in check. Social media has done wonders for communication, but it is emotional suicide when it comes to post-breakup feelings. If you can't stop looking at your ex's profile, then unfollow them, and whatever you do, don't blast your pain all over your various social feeds. Not only will it make you look a little, ahem, unhinged, but it will legitimately make you more miserable in the long run. Trust me, you will be embarrassed later on. You can delete those tweets, but people don't forget! If you're feeling lonely, and absolutely need some emotional validation from strangers and old classmates, instead of plastering every one of your social networks with emo lyrics, ask your followers to help you out by sending you pictures of baby animals cuddling each other. Yeah. Isn't that nice?

5. Distract yourself. Hang out with your friends. Pick up old hobbies. Relationships take a lot of work and time. When you're shifting your schedule to make room for someone else, you have less time to do what you love solo. These sacrifices often go unnoticed. Who wouldn't prefer Friday night fuggles over, well, just about anything else?

6. Did you used to rock climb? Build houses with Habitat for Humanity? Paint with watercolors? Volunteer? Has it been eight months since you made it to your 8 A.M. Saturday morning yoga class? Do you have a half-finished fan fiction novel floating around your hard drive? Get back into whatever made you thrive the last time you were on your own.

7. One of my favorite things to do after a breakup is work on my fitness. Unlike a tequila tasting or your ex's Facebook, working out is a productive distraction. I might wake up listless and mopey, but somewhere around mile three of my run, as I am cruising along to Beyoncé, I start feeling like a bad bitch who doesn't need anyone else to make her feel good. Regardless of whether you're more gym bunny or couch potato, if there is ever a time to get into exercise, it is right after a split. Exercise creates endorphins, which make you happy and improve your confidence. Also, your ass will look even better than it does now. So that can't hurt.

The Break-Up Recipes

Nothing that a little whipped cream to the face can't fix...

"Don't lecture! It won't make you any friends, or lovers. I learned that the hard way." – JESS, VEGAN

Mexican Hot Chocolate-Covered Strawberries

Prep time: 5 minutes | Cook time: 3 minutes | Serves 2 to 4 | GF, SF

The combination of sweet strawberries, creamy chocolate, and a tiny kick of cayenne creates the ultimate trifecta of deliciousness. The pepper will stimulate your blood and the sugar will help you forget your ex. What's his name again?

1 (3-ounce) block semi-sweet dark chocolate, chopped or grated

1/4 teaspoon ground cinnamon

1/8 teaspoon cayenne pepper

1/8 teaspoon salt

1 pound strawberries, cleaned

1. Line a baking sheet with parchment paper and set aside. In a small saucepan, melt the chocolate, stirring with fork or whisk so it melts evenly and doesn't burn. Add the cinnamon, cayenne, and salt. When fully melted, remove from the heat to prevent burning.

2. Holding the strawberries by the stem end, dip them in the melted chocolate, coating them on each side.

3. Place the dipped strawberries on the prepared cookie sheet and refrigerate for at least 30 minutes to set the chocolate, or until ready to serve.

Cherry Cobbler with Cocoa Nibs

Prep time: 20 minutes Cook Time: 30 minutes | Serves 6 | SFO

It was early summer when I was writing out the menu for Wildflower, and cherries were in season. I started thinking up a cherry cobbler recipe, and my intern at the time, Shayla, said "Um, that's a little blue-collar, isn't it?" I was like, "I don't know, is it?" Her eyes confirmed it, so I thought, how can I make this less bourgeois? I know! Add a superfood. To make this soy-free, use a soy-free vegan butter.

FILLING

1 tablespoon vegan butter

6 cups tart cherries, pitted

1 1/3 cup sugar

1 1/2 teaspoons ground cinnamon

1 cup cocoa nibs

Pinch of salt

1/4 cup cornstarch

1/4 cup water

TOPPING

1 1/4 cups all-purpose flour

2 tablespoons brown sugar

1 tablespoon baking powder

4 tablespoons + 1 teaspoon cold butter

1/2 cup almond milk

1 tablespoon unsweetened cocoa powder

1. Preheat the oven to 400°F. Melt the butter in a large saucepan over medium-high heat. Add the cherries, sugar, cinnamon, cocoa nibs, and salt. In a small bowl, whisk together the cornstarch and water. Add the cornstarch slowly to the pan, stirring constantly, and bring to a low boil. Simmer for approximately 5 minutes, or until the mixture begins to thicken and becomes bubbly. Remove from the heat.

2. In a bowl, combine the flour, sugar, and baking powder. With a pastry blender, incorporate 4 tablespoons of the cold butter. Slowly mix in the milk until just incorporated. Set aside.

3. Grease an 8-inch square baking dish with the remaining 1 teaspoon butter, then pour in the filling. Crumble the reserved topping mixture over the filling, covering completely. Dust with cocoa and bake for 25 to 30 minutes. Cool for 5 minutes before serving. Eat the entire thing by yourself, with a spoon, while you whimper over your ex's Facebook profile. Just kidding. Sorta.

3 THINGS YOU DIDN'T KNOW ABOUT COCOA

1. Cocoa nibs (aka cacao nibs) contain a powerful substance called theobromine. This is a central nervous system stimulant that has a similar effect as caffeine, although not quite as powerful. So what I'm saying is, a second slice is like a double soy cappuccino with extra foam. Not really, but you get it.

2. Cocoa is a great source of flavonols, powerful antioxidants that play an important role in circulation. Flavonols also help prevent fatty acids from oxidizing in the bloodstream, and can reduce the risk of blood clots, heart attacks, and strokes. What?! In a pie? Score.

3. Cocoa contains tryptophan, an essential amino acid required for the production of serotonin. Serotonin is like the body's homemade cocaine. Okay, maybe that's a bit much, but the point is, cocoa can help chase the blues away.

Personal Pan Chocolate Pizza

Prep time: 20 minutes | Cook time: 25 minutes | Serves 1 to 4 | SFO

This recipe is from friend, chef, and iEatGrass.com contributor Shadé Ibe. Chocolate never lets you down. Chocolate isn't afraid to meet your mother or go with you to see *The Nutcracker* for the tenth time. It just feels right...every mouthful better than the last. This particular recipe checks off quite a few boxes for me in terms of breakup comfort food potential. First things first, the dish requires very few ingredients, most of which are probably in your pantry. Next, it combines two of my favorite things, chocolate and pizza. Finally, it involves slapping some dough around, which you can imagine is the face of the one who scorned you, thereby exponentially upping the pizza's deliciousness! Use a soy-free vegan butter to make this soy free.

1 pound storebought vegan pizza dough (or the Sweet Dough recipe)

Melted vegan butter, for brushing dough

1 cup vegan chocolate chips or chocolate spread

1 cup sliced strawberries

1 cup mini vegan marshmallows, or sliced large ones

1/4 cup chopped almonds or hazelnuts

1. Preheat the oven to 450°F. Lightly oil a large baking sheet or line it with parchment paper.

2. Roll out the dough into an 8- to 9-inch round and place it on the prepared baking sheet. Brush the dough with melted butter and bake for 20 minutes, until golden. After removing the crust from the oven, immediately top it with chocolate chips or spread. If using chips, allow to melt a bit on the hot dough, and then spread over the center of the crust. Arrange strawberry slices and marshmallows on the pizza and top with the nuts.

3. Bake for 2 minutes, or until the marshmallows are melted. Let the pizza to cool for a few minutes before slicing and serving. And by serving, I mean eating alone in the kitchen at 2 A.M.

Sweet Dough

1 teaspoon active dry yeast

2 tablespoons brown sugar

1/2 cup warm water or almond milk

2 tablespoons melted vegan butter

1 teaspoon salt

2 cups all-purpose flour

1. In a medium-sized bowl, combine the yeast, sugar, and warm water or milk. Stir to mix, then set aside for about 5 minutes. Stir in the butter, salt, and flour, and mix until thoroughly incorporated. Turn the dough onto a lightly-floured surface and knead for 5 minutes.

2. Lightly oil the surface of the dough and place back into the bowl, covering with a tea towel or plastic wrap, and allow to rise in a warm, draft-free location for 1 hour, or until it's doubled in size.

Cranberry-Walnut Cinnamon Rolls

Prep time: 60 minutes | Cook time: 35 minutes | Serves 6 to 8, or one...sniff sniff | SFO

Sometimes (like when you just got dumped), all you want is gluten, and that's fine. We'll forgive you. So will your sinuses and your waist. I have always loved cinnamon rolls, and these puppies take the cake! Or, um, the rolls! The cranberries are tart, the orange zest is sweet, and the fatty crunch of walnuts makes this batch of doughy goodness the perfect distraction from your love life woes. Use a soy-free vegan butter to make this soy-free.

DOUGH

1 (.25-ounce) package active dry yeast

1/2 cup warm water (105 to 110°F)

1/2 cup almond milk, scalded (180°F)

1/3 cup vegan butter, softened at room temperature

1/4 cup sugar

Egg replacer for 1 egg (page 27)

1 teaspoon salt

3 cups all-purpose flour, divided

FILLING

3/4 cup sugar

1/3 cup vegan butter, melted

1/2 teaspoon orange zest, finely minced

3/4 cup dried cranberries

1/2 cup walnuts, crushed

1 tablespoon ground cinnamon

ICING

2 cups confectioners' sugar

4 tablespoons vegan butter, melted

1 teaspoon vanilla extract

1 teaspoon orange zest

3 to 6 tablespoons hot water

1. Dough: In a small bowl, dissolve the yeast in the warm water and set aside.

2. In a separate bowl, combine the milk, butter, sugar, egg replacer, and salt. Mix well. Add 1 1/2 cups of the flour and mix well. Pour in the yeast and water mixture, and continue mixing. Add the remaining flour and fold to combine.

3. On a lightly floured surface, knead the dough into a ball for 5 to 10 minutes. Tranfer to a lightly-oiled bowl, cover with a clean tea towel or plastic wrap, and set aside for 1 1/2 hours, until doubled in size.

4. Punch down your dough and roll it out into a 15x9-inch rectangle. Grease a 9-inch round baking pan and set aside.

5. Filling: In a small bowl, combine the sugar and melted butter. Stir in the zest and spread the mixture onto the top of the dough, leaving a 1/2-inch margin on all sides. Sprinkle evenly with the cranberries, walnuts, and cinnamon. Roll up the dough lengthwise. Pinch the ends closed.

6. Slice the dough into 8 to 10 wheels and transfer them to the prepared pan, cut-side down. Cover and let rest at room temperature for 45 minutes. Preheat the oven to 350°F. Bake for 30 minutes, or until golden brown.

7. Icing: In a small bowl, mix the powdered sugar, melted butter, vanilla, and orange zest. Add water by the tablespoon until the icing becomes thin and drizzly. Drizzle the icing on the cinnamon rolls and serve warm.

Spiced Peach and Plum Cobbler

Prep time: 10 minutes | Cook time: 60 minutes | Serves 6 to 8 | SFO

I grew up with two plum trees in my backyard, and I was thinking about those summers when I would go climb the tree to get a pocket full of plums to munch on while I roamed around the neighborhood with a slingshot in my back pocket and some handlebars in my hand. They were the best candy I could have had. I revisited them a couple of summers ago when I went home while dealing with some heartache and after an ice storm the previous winter tore up most of the trees in my parents' backyard. A little known fact: plum trees have a very strong and intricate root system. And so, like every summer, we had an abundance of plums and a few peaches lying around. I asked my father if he'd ever had a plum cobbler. He said no, so we made one, talked about how Ginger reminded him of one of his ex–girlfriends, and ate cobbler and ice cream. Use soy-free vegan butter to make this soy-free. Note: You can make this in a pie pan, if you prefer.

FILLING

1 tablespoon vegan butter

2 to 3 ripe peaches, pitted and sliced

3 to 4 ripe plums, pitted and sliced

1 cup granulated sugar

1 teaspoon ground cinnamon

1/2 teaspoon ground nutmeg

1/4 teaspoon allspice

1 teaspoon vanilla extract

Pinch of salt

1/4 cup cornstarch

2 tablespoons water

2 teaspoons fresh lemon juice

CRUST

Double the crust recipe from Devil's Pot
    Pie, page 80

1. Preheat the oven to 400°F. Melt the butter in a medium skillet over medium heat. Add the peaches, plums, sugar, cinnamon, nutmeg, allspice, vanilla, and salt. Lower the heat to medium-low and sauté for approximately 5 minutes, stirring constantly.

2. In a small bowl, combine the cornstarch with the water and lemon juice. Whisk until smooth. Add to the fruit mixture and simmer, stirring, until it thickens, 3 to 5 minutes. Remove from the heat.

3. Roll out the dough for the bottom crust on waxed parchment paper. Fit the rolled-out dough into the bottom of an 8-inch shallow baking dish, and pour in the reserved filling.

4. Roll out the remaining dough and cut it into strips. Arrange the strips on top of the filling in a lattice pattern (alternating strips at 90 degree angles, spaced about 1/2-inch apart).

5. Bake for 50 to 60 minutes, or until the crust is golden brown and the filling is bubbling. Let it rest for a few minutes before serving.

Pro-tip: Before baking, brush the crust with vegan butter for a nice golden brown finish. If your oven is known for cooking unevenly, cover the edges of the cobbler with foil to prevent over-browning until the last 5 minutes of baking.

Cardamom Chia Seed Parfait

Prep time: 5 minutes +overnight | Serves 2 to 4 | SF

I discovered chia seed in a horrible way—in a drink. It's nutritious, but it gelatinizes in a way that I think is off-putting in a beverage. However, this experience made me realize its potential as a thickener, so at least something good came out of that minor trauma. I served this pudding for raw night at one of my pop-ups, and it was a hit! I re-imagined it as a parfait so I could eat dessert for breakfast, as one often does when recently dumped. No? Just me?

2 cups almond milk

1 cup raw cashews

2 tablespoons brown sugar

1 teaspoon ground cardamom

1/8 teaspoon salt

3 tablespoons chia seeds

1 cup of your favorite granola

Fresh blueberries, for topping

1. In a blender, combine the almond milk, cashews, sugar, cardamom, and salt. Blend until completely smooth.

2. Pour the mixture into a large mason jar. Stir in the chia seeds, mixing well. Cover and place in the refrigerator until the next morning.

3. Assemble in parfait glasses or dessert bowls from bottom to top: a layer of granola, a layer of pudding, another layer of granola, more pudding, then top with fresh blueberries.

Peach Pie Popsicles

Prep time: 5 minutes | Serves 4 to 6 | GF, SF

This recipe was an absolute fluke. I was making a smoothie one day with two old peaches and whatever else was in the fridge. I drank half the smoothie and thought, "You know what? This would be great as a popsicle." I had no popsicle sticks, but I had a spoon. I stuck the spoon in the cup and put it in the freezer. It came out delicious, like a peach pie on a stick. You can't go wrong with this.

1 cup almond milk

1 frozen banana, peeled and chopped

2 large peaches, pitted and diced

1/2 teaspoon pure vanilla extract

1 tablespoon agave nectar

Pinch of ground cinnamon

1. Combine all ingredients in a blender and blend until smooth.

2. Pour into a popsicle tray and freeze until set, 3 to 6 hours.

Strawberry Shortcakes

Prep time: 10 minutes | Cook time: 15 minutes | Serves 1 to 2

These are quick, easy, and fattening—guaranteed to cheer anyone up from the lowest of lows. Light, fluffy biscuits, whipped cream, and fresh strawberries are a no brainer.

1 cup all-purpose flour

1/2 tablespoon baking powder

1/2 teaspoon sea salt

2 tablespoons vegan butter, very cold

1/2 cup almond milk

1 cup vegan Soya Too whipped cream
   or coconut cream

2 cups sliced strawberries

1. In a medium bowl, combine the flour, baking powder, and salt. Mix well. Using a fork or pastry blender, cut in the cold butter. Slowly add the milk, gradually stirring until the dough pulls away from the side of the bowl.

2. Place the dough onto a floured surface and knead 15 to 20 times. Pat or roll the dough out to a 1-inch thickness. Cut biscuits with a large cookie cutter or the top of a juice glass dipped in flour. Repeat until all dough is used. Brush off the excess flour, and place the biscuits onto an ungreased baking sheet. Bake for 13 to 15 minutes.

3. Split the baked and cooled biscuits in half. Place one half of a sliced biscuit on a plate or in the bottom of a bowl. Top with a dollop of whipped cream and some strawberries, then place the remaining biscuit half atop the strawberries. Add another dollop of whipped cream and top with more strawberries.

"Of course we taste better..."

Getting over someone sucks. It effin' hurts. After you distract yourself with busy work, and put on all the "I'm okay" smiles to your friends, you still have to go home to an half-empty apartment, half-empty kitchen, and half-empty bed. Even on the rare occasions you have a drunken sleepover with some co-worker who likes you way more than you like them, it just makes you mad, because they don't sleep in the bed the right way and their neck nuzzle is all wrong. You feel a little guilty, and a little like a jerk, and a lot like crying...in a grown-up way, of course.

AYINDÉ: After Ginger, I told myself I would never date an omnivore again. If they're not vegan, no chance! But alas, no luck. That was when I really learned what I covered in the first few chapters—veganism is just one piece of the puzzle. I also want a woman who is smart, funny, quick-witted, subtly sexy, and feminine. It's hard to find someone who is all of that, and vegan, and single, and free of major diseases, and interested in all-a-dis right here. So I did what other normal humans do: try and move on by having flings and hook-ups, not caring if they're vegan as long as they're down. Why? To ease the pain! Remember when I said it effin' hurts? Well, it still does. No matter how bad the pain is, when you're rebounding, try not to do the following things.

What not to do on the rebound

The Under-Over. The under-over, also known as the U/O, is the idea that you have to get UNDER someone new to get OVER the ex. There is no feeling for this person, and you screw like you don't care. And you do this a couple times to get their essence all on you, and then you drop them cold. No feelings. It's best done in a one night stand or drunken late night booty-call format. The under-over is a dirty, self-serving thing to do, you asshole. Do not do it, and if you do, it should only be used as a Hail Mary. If you've already tried everything your therapist told you, like all of it, then maybe the U/O is a last resort. If you have to do it, definitely avoid anyone who may potentially like you and want more. And don't spend the night. If you start spending the night, you will get too comfy, your brain will release oxytocin, creating a love bond, and all of a sudden you're dating someone you didn't like in the first place, and you did it to yourself.

The Doppelbang. You're out one night chatting up a hottie, and you realize this person looks and talks just like your ex! They even kind of smell like them! Your brain is sighing in relief. Back slowly away. And then run. If you are so hung up on your ex, just call 'em up! Ask yourself, "Why am I about to ruin this person's week, just because I like Libras, and I'm not over the last one?" It ain't right! This is your mantra: "I don't even really like you anyway!"

Okay, so now I told you two things not to do. I know what you're saying. "But Ayindé, if I can't have one-night stands and sleep with people who look just like my ex, what can I do?"

Well, I'll tell you.

What you should do on the rebound

Learn how to cook! Cooking releases creative energy, and it will give you something to focus on. Without your ex, you now have all of this time on your hands, right? Why not use it to gain a skill set that will surely impress whomever comes along next? If you bought this book, you're at least partially interested in becoming a better cook. Bonus: your friends will be more likely to listen to you complain about how the chick you met at Whole Foods smelled like a perfect wildflower,

but silly you, you didn't ask for her number, if they're smiling and nodding with their mouths full of your great home cookin'—everybody's happy. So be productive and creative. You always meet people when you're elbows deep doing your thing. The perfect place to meet other vegans is in the grocery store. No meat in the basket means go for it!

Disconnect Online. It might seem like it's not a big deal, but you can't really break up with someone these days if you are constantly seeing them all over your timelines or mutual friends' timelines. Ginger was never that into social media, but once we broke up, she not only unfriended me, but somehow orchestrated a total friends and family blackout. She took all her friends back, and, just like that, she was gone. Like gone, gone. After that last day in Fort Greene in Brooklyn. I don't even know what her hair looks like these days. She was going natural, but I have no idea now. In the end, I think it was best to help get past the painful parts, but damn if that unfriended notice didn't sting.

ZOË: After my split with Daniel and my social binge-fest, my body didn't feel too good. I was sleeping less, which meant I was tired—too tired to make healthful eating decisions. French fries may be vegan, but they didn't make me feel good once I licked my fingers free of ketchup and salt. Six months post-split, just as I was starting to think seriously about dating again, I realized my jeans didn't fit anymore. I started focusing on healthier eating to get my body back into peak performance. As I did so, my sex drive had a bit of a reawakening.

Food and sex have long been correlated. Eating is sensual, after all. I remember during the first six months of dating, I was really into watching Daniel eat ice cream cones. D-d-d-dairy ice cream cones. What on earth could make a vegan girl want to watch someone eat a dairy ice cream cone? It was all in the tongue.

I've always been a bit of a voyeur, and watching my boyfriend tongue anything with that much interest was hot. But the feeling also came with a side of guilt. I don't agree with eating dairy, so that felt sort of gross. Plus, since I was watching and not eating, I felt like an adult taking a child out for an ice-cream cone. This made me feel like a Humbert Humbert-style pervert, except my Lolita was not a fourteen-year-old girl, but a twenty-something man with an ice cream cone. Everyone likes a dirty girl. Right? Right!?! What I'm saying is, I had a lady boner. I sat there going, pretend it's soy, pretend it's soy, pretend it's soy...

If the ice cream incident taught me anything, it's that eating can be a sexual, sensual experience. But for two people who love to babble about food and sex, you may be surprised to learn that Ayindé and I don't really believe in aphrodisiacs. Unless you count tequila.

Why vegans have better sex

While I don't think any specific food is going to make you immediately want to take your clothes off, I do believe there are nutritional components found in certain foods that will make your body and organs perform better or worse—sex organs included. Not sure what I mean? When's the last time you said, "That third helping of Chinese food really made me want to f*ck." Yeah, that's what I thought.

FOOD AND SEX
HAVE LONG BEEN CORRELATED.
EATING IS SENSUAL, AFTER ALL.

I really hate to generalize, but as a whole, vegans tend to be a healthier lot than the average American. Healthier individuals tend to have better-maintained bodily systems than their not-so-healthy counterparts, and what is your libido if not a finely tuned bodily system? Of course, "vegan" is not synonymous with "healthy," but if you're eating a plant-based diet rich in whole grains, legumes, and veggies, and limiting processed foods and artificial fillers, then you're most likely having better sex than those whose bodies are weighed down by animal products. Let's talk about why.

Those following a vegan diet tend to have...

More energy. An increase in energy is usually one of the first things people notice when they go vegan. Veganism is like crack. Healthy, inexpensive crack, without that jittery, tweaked-out feeling or the disapproving family members. I have no idea what I am talking about here; I've never done crack, I just watch a lot of movies. But really, you go vegan, and you feel energized. This is because those of us on plant-based, whole-foods diets are eating foods that are easier to digest, allowing us to have more energy to dedicate to other activities. Like boning.

Boosted libidos. "Libido" is just a fun label for your overall sex drive. Because we're an instant-gratification culture, most of us falsely believe that aphrodisiacs make you want to have sex directly after eating them. The actual definition of an aphrodisiac is a food that increases your sexual desire. It's not instantaneous, folks. Like most dietary changes, you have to keep at it to see results. I haven't yet found a food that, upon eating, made me want to have sex. However, I have found that certain foods make me feel better, and by better, I mean, like having more sex.

Scientific research has revealed that certain foods cause a chemical reaction in the human body that can amp up our libido. Luckily for all of us grass eaters, the majority of the foods that keep your body in peak sexual condition are plant-based. We run down tons of libidinous plant-based foods later in the chapter so you can be sure to stock your arsenal with bonerific eats. In addition to our list, a good rule of thumb is to look for foods with lots of zinc and vitamin B, which supposedly elevate testosterone levels and increase desire for both genders.

Improved taste and smell. What you eat directly affects the way you taste and smell. Meat and dairy are acidic and hard for your body to digest, and this can create an acrid scent and flavor on

your person. Your, ahem, entire person. Need proof? Think about what happens twenty minutes after you eat asparagus. Yep, I went there.

We worked up the gall to ask many of our friends to give us the tasty details about their past lovers, and they all had stories about the difference in flavor and scent between vegans and omnis. If that research isn't scientific enough for ya, then chew on this: a 2006 study published in the journal Chemical Senses found body odor when on a plant-based diet was significantly more attractive and "less intense" than on an omnivorous diet.

I'm not sure what "less intense" means, but I can only imagine it means less offensive. The study directly noted that red meat consumption has a negative impact on perceived body odor. Unfortunately, the study didn't have a taste-testing component, and we found it hard to secure a grant for that kind of research. Seriously, we asked. (No, we didn't.) However, since our sense of taste and smell are directly correlated, well, the findings would most likely have crossed over. Mind you, it's not just animal products that affect your flavor. Those who eat diets heavy in pungent foods like onion, garlic, chives, and leeks often have more acrid-tasting sexbits and ejaculate, as well as sharper body odor overall.

Increased natural lubrications. Many plant-based foods (see our list below for specifics) naturally increase lubrication in women. These include water-rich foods that hydrate you, as well as munchies that are rich in omega-3 fatty acids, which help improve the overall health of skin and mucus membranes (ew, sorry, I know).

Increased blood flow. A vegan diet helps clear the plaque off your arterial walls, allowing blood to flow directly to the places it matters. Men, this means achieving and sustaining an erection will be easier. Women, this means you will find yourself stimulated faster. So the next time you have a triple round of O's, you can roll over and say "Thank you, soluble fiber!"

Did you know that diet heavy in animal products is typically also heavy in synthetic hormones? This can lead to a reduction in sperm count! If you want healthy swimmers, go organic and plant-based. (Note: I am not suggesting a meaty diet as a form of birth control. Whew, that would be an awfully ridiculous lawsuit.)

Lower levels of stress. According to a 2012 study published in the Nutrition Journal, meat-free folks tend to be happier and less stressed than those who munch on mammals. Happier people tend to be having more sex overall. Also, polyphenols (compounds found in plant-based foods) can positively affect brain cognition, making you happier and calmer. In a nearly 10-year survey published in the Nutritional Neuroscience journal in 2012, researchers found that greater fruit and vegetable intake correlated with lower odds of mood disorders like depression and chronic anxiety. I don't want to speak for everybody here, but heightened anxiety doesn't usually lead to heightened orgasms...if that were the case, more of us would be having sex right before standardized tests and doctor visits. Now there's a waiting room I would like to be in...

Boosted confidence. There isn't any scientific evidence proving that a vegan diet enhances sexual attractiveness, since that's all in the eye of the beholder. However, the better care we take of our bodies, the better we tend to look and feel, and the more time we want to spend naked.

Are you having sex with animals?

Even seasoned vegans often forget to check their personal products for animal ingredients before sexpressing themselves; you don't want to be unknowingly slathering your bits and pieces with animals, do you? (Now there's an image I bet you didn't want.)

If you (or your partner) like it veggie-style, then this is for you. Here is a breakdown of exactly what is in those condoms and lubes that keep them from being vegan. We'll also let you know where you can find alternatives and give you a list of our favorite Lusty Vegan-approved products that are not only good for animals and your holiest of holies, but for the planet, too! Let's put the passion in compassion, people!

Here are some reasons your sexy stuff may not be vegan:

Latex: Latex is the sap of the rubber tree. Sounds great, right? Unfortunately not. The latex found in most condoms and some sex toys is often manufactured with casein, a milk protein. However, cruelty-free companies have been researching alternatives for years now, and have come up with a process of replacing casein with a vegetable extract from the thistle family. Thank goodness!

Lambskin condoms: Do I even need to explain here? Fine. Lambskin condoms were thought up as an alternative for those who are allergic to latex. Lambskin condoms are made from a thin layer of sheep cecum—a part of the intestine. Yum.

Oral contraceptives: This is controversial for many lady vegans who don't want to contribute to animal testing, but also don't want to get pregnant. Or maybe they have a health condition that is treated by oral contraceptives. Unfortunately, as of 2014, no oral birth control is vegan. As required by the FDA, they are all tested on animals. Plus, many of the pills include lactose, a milk by-product. There is an environmental issue here too. Hormonal birth control contains synthetic estrogen and progesterone, which have been shown to have an effect on aquatic animals when they are excreted into our water system. Gross, right? Just another thing to think about.

Animal testing: Just because your fave product doesn't contain animal products (woo!), that doesn't mean it's cruelty-free (boo). For instance, Trojan claims their condoms are free of animal byproducts, but their manufacturers, Church & Dwight, test on animals.

Lubricants: Many personal lubes contain animal ingredients, from honey to the dairy-derived enzyme lactoperoxidase. (Say that five times fast.)

As consumers smarten up to what's going in and on their goods, more and more conscious companies are surfacing, and that's fantastic. Some of our favorites are Sliquid, Glyde, Sir Richard's, Good Clean Love, and RFSU.

Stories from the Field

Hayley Marie Norman, actress, model, activist

"Veganism has impacted my romantic relationships in both a positive and negative way. Negative in the sense that it seems a lot of people tend to get intimidated when they hear that I'm vegan. They automatically assume that vegans are holier-than-thou health nuts with no vices who have no fun and take pleasure in making the other party feel guilty about their food choices. I have to say, this is probably in some ways a positive as well, because if someone is going to be intimidated by something like veganism, then they aren't strong enough to handle me anyway, and it was never going to work. One positive impact veganism has had on dating is that it's become a much quicker way for me to suss someone out or get a more accurate sense of their worldview. If someone scoffs at veganism or my love for the environment or animals, I know immediately that this is an individual that is most likely not capable of seeing a bigger worldview picture outside of themselves. As corny as that sounds, I know I need to be with someone who wants to leave this world a better place than they found it, and is willing to sacrifice a few creature comforts here and there for someone or something else."

Food for Sex: The Pantry

What are some of these foods that will prime your organs for optimum O's? Let's run down the list of a few of our feel-good faves and what they do to our bodies to keep us nice and juicy.

- The Aztecs named the avocado tree the "testicle tree," most likely due to the fact that they grow in pairs. The heart-healthy fats in these creamy fruits keep your blood flowing to all of the right places. Plus, the monounsaturated fats can ward of heart disease, and men with heart disease are twice as likely to suffer from E.D. (yes, that dysfunction). Yikes!

- Blueberries have been said to be one of the best foods for guys suffering from E.D., because they have lots of soluble fiber, which can help clear arteries. They also can relax your uppity blood vessels and improve circulation. All of these things can lead to boners abound. How's that for word-foreplay?

- As if you needed another reason to eat chocolate, cocoa is packed with antioxidants, which will keep you healthy all over. But it also contains phenylethylamine, which stimulates a sense of excitement and boosts your mood. If you're opting for chocolate over raw cocoa, remember that the darker the better, as it will have less sugar and higher cocoa ratios.

- Kale, spinach, collards, and so on are blood-purifying foods that enhance circulation and can speed up stimulation. More greens, please!

- Spicy foods can speed up your metabolism and increase blood flow. And you know what I mean when I say blood flow.

- I know soy gets a bad name, but it's actually full of phytoestrogens that keep those girly parts well-lubricated. And we all like our girly parts well-lubricated. Take that!

- All hail beta carotene! The vibrant orange of sweet potatoes is a vitamin A precursor giveaway, and vitamin A is an important generator for sex hormone production. Ladies, it also keeps the vaginal and uterine walls healthy. Carrots can do this, too, but sweet potatoes taste better with ketchup.

Okay, now that we've covered the do's and don'ts and you've restocked your sex cabinet, you're ready to get back in the game. But first, let's get back in the kitchen. Remember the best way to meet people is through friends, so call up some homies and let them know that you're single *and* you can cook.

Food for Sex

Eating is sensual, after all

"Vegans taste better—this I know for sure. As in, down there. Yeah, that's right. You taste better when you don't eat animals or their secretions. This is a scientific factoid that most vegans are clued into." – CHLOÉ JO DAVIS, FOUNDER/OWNER, GIRLIE GIRL ARMY

Pan-Seared Asparagus with Caramelized Ginger

Prep time: 5 minutes | Cook time: 7 minutes | Serves: 2 | GF, SF

I was afraid to eat asparagus when I was kid, mainly because I didn't know how to prepare it. As an adult and professional chef, I played around with it amd I realized that asparagus is great solo, but even better when highlighted with accents of spicy ginger. The simple seasoning really brings this dish to life.

2 tablespoons grapeseed or safflower oil

2 tablespoons ginger, peeled and sliced into 2-inch strips

1 pound asparagus, woody stems removed

1/2 teaspoon coarse sea salt or smoked salt

Ground white pepper

1. Heat the oil in a large skillet over medium-high heat. Add the ginger and reduce the heat to medium-low until the ginger is caramelized, 5 to 7 minutes. Remove the ginger from the skillet with a slotted spoon and set aside in a small bowl.

2. Add the asparagus to the hot pan and cook until golden on all sides. Sprinkle the asparagus with salt and pepper. Remove from heat, and serve topped with the caramelized ginger.

Pro-tip: The smoked sea salt and white pepper give it a unique flavor, but if you don't feel like making a trip to the store, use what you have on hand. Be fancy some other time!

Oven-Roasted Brussels Sprouts with Medjool Dates

Prep time: 8 minutes | Cook time: 25 minutes | Serves 4 to 6 | GF, SF

India.Arie is a big fan of Brussels sprouts, and I am a big fan of matching flavors. The natural bitterness of the sprouts really pops when matched with the sweet creamy consistency of dates and the sharp spiciness of garlic. The complex combination makes this dish satisfying on a lot of levels. It's a great addition to any meal as a side, and for Brussels sprouts lovers, it's a whole meal.

1 (10-ounce) package shaved Brussels sprouts (see Pro-tip)

2 cups pitted dates, torn into quarters

3 tablespoons grapeseed or safflower oil

1 teaspoon coarse salt

1 teaspoon black pepper

6 cloves garlic, peeled and sliced

1. Preheat the oven to 400°F. In a 9 x 13-inch baking dish combine the Brussels sprouts and dates with the oil, salt, and pepper. Toss to make sure all the pieces of dates and Brussels sprouts are covered evenly. Sprinkle the garlic on top.

2. Roast for 20 minutes or until the garlic has caramelized and the dates and Brussels sprouts have browned on top.

Pro-tip: If you cannot find shaved Brussels sprouts, take the Brussels sprout and cut from top to bottom; lay flat and then slice thin shreds as if it were an onion.

Flash-Sautéed Kale

Prep time: 5 minutes | Cook time: 5 minutes | Serves 2 | GF, SF

My client India.Arie's favorite green was kale, so after a year on tour, I have a pretty big kale dish list. Personally, I cannot get raw kale out of my teeth, which is annoying. Luckily, this salad is easy on the chompers and very flavorful. Enjoy!

2 tablespoons grapeseed or safflower oil

4 whole cloves garlic

4 cups kale, chopped

2 tablespoons lemon juice

1/2 teaspoon coarse salt

1/2 teaspoon black pepper

1 tablespoon hemp hearts

Lemon wedges, to serve

1. Heat the oil in a large skillet over medium-high heat until shimmering. Add the garlic and sauté until brown on both sides, about 1 minute.

2. Add the kale, mixing from the bottom, and incorporating all of it into the hot oil. Add the lemon juice, salt, and pepper. Cover and reduce the heat to medium. Cook for 2 minutes. Remove from the heat, garnish with hemp hearts, and serve with wedge of lemon.

Pro-Tip: You can easily add some oyster mushrooms to this recipe and make it a great complete meal. To do so, just toss them in with the garlic and sauté away!

WTF are hemp hearts? Hemp hearts are shelled hemp seeds. They are a superfood full of protein and essential fatty acids, good for the brain, skin, and—you guessed it—sex drive. Their nutty flavor makes them a tasty addition to most dishes, so if you buy a bag for this recipe, trust that you will be sprinkling them onto many other things, too.

Polenta Cakes
with Chili-Garlic Sauce

Prep time: 8 minutes | Cook time: 10 minutes | Serves 2 | GF, SF

I love the texture of corn polenta. While creating a restaurant menu, I came up with a quinoa cake similar to this. However, I later swapped in polenta, because I find the grain to be heartier in this dish. The addition of chili-garnic sauce is guaranteed to get the blood circulating to all the right parts. Enjoy!

2 tablespoons grapeseed or safflower oil, divided

1/4 cup finely chopped onion

1/4 cup finely chopped green bell pepper

2 teaspoons minced fresh rosemary

1 teaspoon dried basil

1 teaspoon garlic powder

1/4 teaspoon cayenne

1/4 teaspoon red pepper flakes

1 1/2 cup water

1/2 cup dry corn polenta

1/2 teaspoon salt

1/4 cup unsweetened almond milk

Chili-garlic sauce, to serve

1. Heat 1 tablespoon of the oil in a medium skillet over medium-high heat until hot. Add the onion and bell pepper and sauté for approximately 4 minutes, until the onion becomes translucent.

2. Add the rosemary, basil, garlic powder, cayenne, and red pepper flakes and sauté for an additional 3 to 4 minutes. Remove from the heat.

3. Heat the water in a medium saucepan until boiling. Add the polenta and salt, whisking to incorporate and smooth out lumps. Reduce the heat to medium-low and allow to cook for 3 to 5 minutes. The polenta will start to thicken. Add the almond milk and mix well with a whisk. Remove from heat once the mixture has thickened. Fold the sautéed veggies into the polenta and mix until well combined.

4. Pour the mixture into a lightly oiled 8-inch square baking dish and refrigerate until firm, 8 to 10 minutes.

5. Once the polenta has cooled and firmed, cut the polenta into triangles and flash-grill it in a hot skillet with the remaining 1 tablespoon of oil. Cook until lightly browned on both sides, approximately 3 minutes. Serve with chili-garlic sauce.

North African Lentil Stew
with Roasted Yams

Prep time: 8 minutes | Cook time: 35 to 40 minutes | Serves 2 | GF, SF

This hearty recipe was created with both male and female reproductive systems in mind. Lentils are good for men's reproductive health, and sweet potatoes for women's reproductive systems. Here, I combined them both with North African flavors, adding peanuts for a protein boost and a topping of fresh cilantro to round it all out.

1 medium yam or sweet potato

1 tablespoon plus 1 teaspoon grapeseed or safflower oil, divided

2 cups water

3/4 cup uncooked French lentils

1 leek, white and light green parts only,
   cut into wheels

1/4 cup chopped onion

1/4 cup diced bell pepper

1/2 cup roasted peanuts

1 tablespoon chopped ginger

2 teaspoon ground cumin

1 teaspoon smoked paprika

1/2 teaspoon red pepper flakes

1/2 teaspoon salt, or more to taste

1/2 teaspoon habanero or ghost pepper, minced and seeded (optional;
   see Note)

1 cup unsweetened almond or coconut
   milk

1 tablespoon chopped fresh cilantro,
   for garnish

1. Preheat the oven to 350°F. Cut the yam in half lengthwise. Place the yam halves in a baking dish, cut-side up, and brush each half with 1/2 teaspoon of oil. Bake until fork tender and golden brown around edges, approximately 30 minutes.

2. While the yam is are baking, bring 2 cup water to a boil in a small saucepan. Add the lentils and reduce the heat to medium-low. Cook the lentils until tender, 25 to 30 minutes.

3. In a medium skillet over medium-high heat, heat the 1 table-spoon of oil until hot and shimmering. Add the leeks, onion, and bell pepper, and sauté until the onion becomes translucent, 3 to 5 minutes.

4. Add the peanuts, ginger, cumin, paprika, red pepper flakes, salt, and habanero (if using), stirring well. Sauté for an additional 2 to 3 minutes.

5. Add the cooked lentils and almond milk and mix well. Reduce to a simmer on medium-low heat for 7 to 10 minutes. Remove from the heat. Serve the lentil mixture hot over the yams. Garnish with cilantro.

Note: If you use these chile peppers, cut them with plastic gloves on and know that they are hot as shit. The ghost pepper is also called the king cobra of peppers, so let that inform you.

Kale-oritos

Prep time: 5 minutes | Cook time: 18 minutes | Serves 1 to 2 | GF, SFO

Every vegan must have a great kale chip recipe, and I haven't left you hanging. If you love kale chips and heat, these guys are guaranteed to satisfy. This is an oven recipe, but if you own a dehydrator, you can set it to 110°F and dehydrate overnight. Omit the vegan Parmesan from the seasoning mix to make these treats completely raw. This seasoning blend is also fantastic on popcorn! Use a soy-free vegan Parmesan to make this soy-free.

1/4 cup nutritional yeast

2 tablespoons vegan Parmesan

1 tablespoon smoked paprika

2 teaspoons dried basil

1 teaspoon ground turmeric

1/4 teaspoon cayenne

2 1/2 cups packed kale leaves, stems removed (about 5 ounces)

2 tablespoons olive oil

Salt

1. Preheat oven to 350°F. In a small bowl, combine the nutritional yeast, parmesan, smoked paprika, basil, turmeric, and cayenne. Mix well.

2. In a medium bowl, toss the kale in the olive oil. Add 3 tablespoons of seasoning mixture and toss until all the kale is evenly covered in oil and seasoning.

3. Spread the kale onto a baking sheet and bake until crispy, mixing and turning about half way through to prevent burning, 15 to 18 minutes. If your oven has hot spots, you can turn the entire tray once to prevent burning.

Pro-tip: Be sure not to leave any of the stems in the kale leaves, or you will burn your chips waiting for the stems to cook.

Arugula and Barley Pomegranate Salad

Prep time: 5 minutes | Serves: 2 to 4 | GF, SF

Just like asparagus, arugula is also a veggie that lies off the beaten path. Its subtle spice makes you either love it or put it down forever the first time you try it. This salad was used in another of my pop-ups, Gourmand in Brooklyn. The combination of the spicy arugula and tart pomegranate really pops, but you may have to chase your pom seeds around the plate. That's just part of the experience.

DRESSING

1/4 cup extra-virgin olive oil

2 tablespoons white balsamic vinegar

1 tablespoon chickpea miso paste

1 tablespoon maple syrup

2 teaspoons dried basil

1/2 teaspoon salt

1/4 teaspoon red pepper flakes

1/4 teaspoon minced fresh rosemary

SALAD

1 (5-ounce) bag baby arugula

1/2 cup pomegranate seeds

1/2 cup shredded red cabbage

1. Dressing: Combine all the dressing ingredients in a bowl and use a fork or whisk to blend until smooth.

2. Salad: In a bowl, combine the arugula, pomegranate seeds, and cabbage. Add the dressing and toss to combine. Serve immediately.

10. HACK THIS BOOK

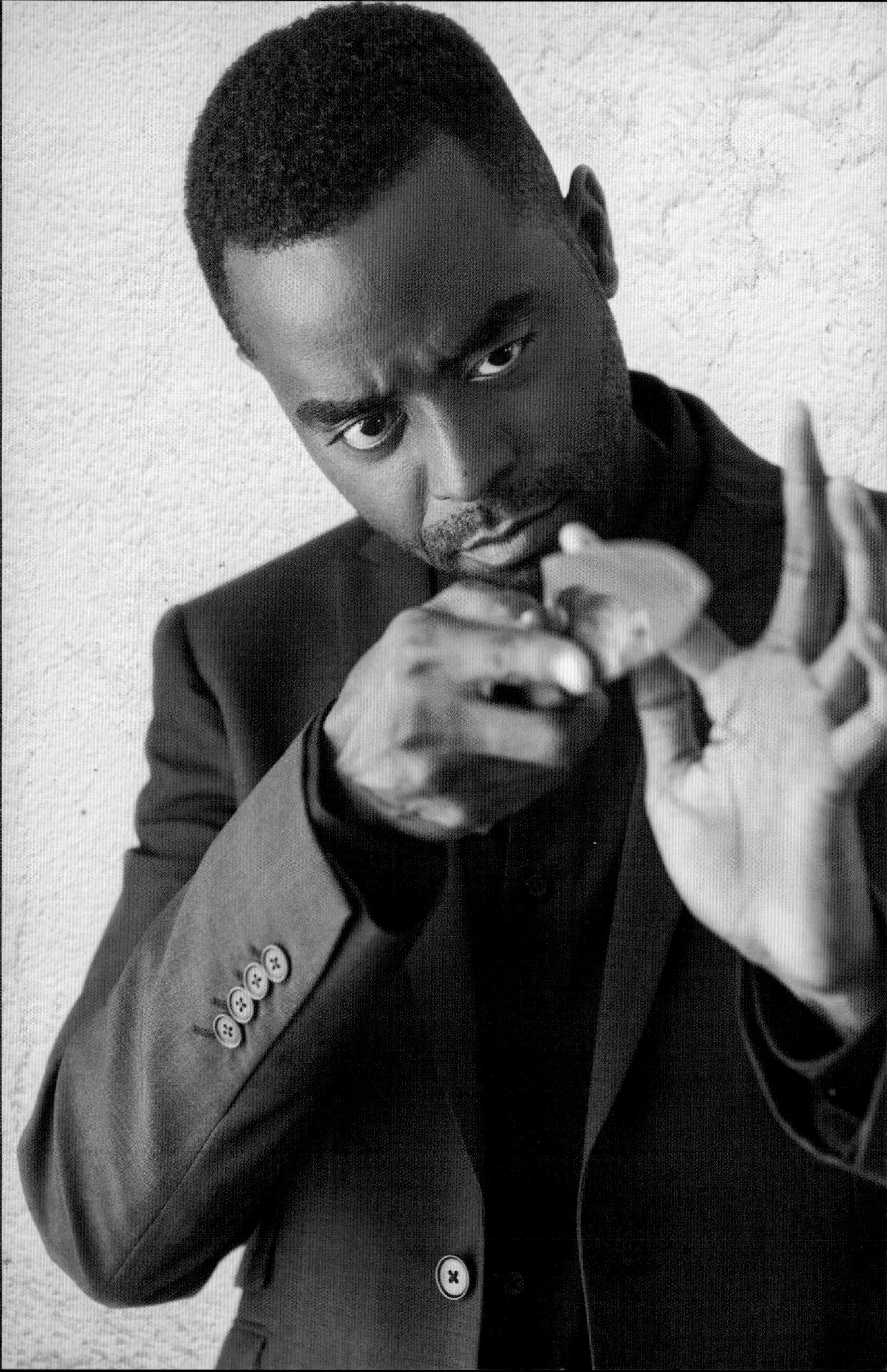

Kitchen Hacks: Recipe Remixes

The book is coming to a close, but no need to pout. We still have one final chapter to run through. In this chapter, we're going to tell you what to do with your leftovers. Sure, sometimes you just want to eat them cold out of the fridge, but, more often, you want to try to make use of what you've already got. These "hacks" are perfect the day after a Lusty Vegan party, for those late night cravings, or a TV binge-watching weekend.

AYINDE: I came up with the recipes in this chapter while testing other recipes for this book. I was working on all of the dishes at the same time, and I live alone. This meant a lot of leftovers in the fridge. After testing and eating them again and again, eventually I got restless, because, well, I'm mildly ADD. However, in this scenario, my ADD was a good thing, because I started remixing leftovers, and this chapter was born. From sauces to seasonings, the ultimate holiday wrap, and epic biscuits and gravy, this chapter covers the basic things I want in my face quickly when I walk into my kitchen after a long day of work.

When I use the word "hack," I don't mean all of these recipes are easy. Actually, remixing recipes and thinking off the page is advanced stuff. These hacks reference other recipes and are only easy if you are prepared. If the Seitan was your midterm, then this is the final. So think like a pro—or at least a reality show contestant—and prep your ingredients first. I don't want you flipping or swiping back and forth in the book, because timing is always key in cooking.

Many of these hacks will help you reinvent what's already laying around in the fridge. You'll actually be creating whole new dishes from this book by adding something leftover to the mix! It's for the experimental and adventurous among you. Once you get the hang of how this hacking works, I think you will be hacking the mess out of this book. A beautiful mess of course. So, if hindsight is 20/20, you'll remember the good times when you look back on relationships, and remember the great recipes when you look back on this book.

This food hacker chapter is great for one of those nights when you're looking at what you have in the fridge and you want something new, but you don't want to cook again. Well, using the below kitchen hacking skillz, you will learn how to act like a kid again and choose your own kitchen adventure. I formulated these hacks for leftovers, but after much thought, I am writing them as if you are starting from scratch with an empty fridge. That way, we can all be on the same page. However, if you have leftovers, skip the recipes portion and simply reheat and assemble.

Depending on the recipe, I will, from time to time, suggest you make something the night before, like your proteins and sauces, i.e., seitan, or any of the seasoned quinoas or tofu. That way you will save time again—crucial for hacking.

In these hack recipes, I often tell you to make half recipes, which means you need to divide the measurements in half, but you still follow the technique just the same. It's called math. Cool? So, let the hacking and recipe remixing begin! Wiki wiki.

Hack This Book

Recipe remixes and food extensions

"There's no need to be nasty or forceful. People see the changes in your health and your positive light shining and they want some of it too! My husband is omni, and while I cook us vegan food, I try hard to respect his wishes and wants to live his life his way. As much as I would love him to be Vegan, driving it home every day that I am the one who is "right" will only make him possibly love me less."
– AMARIE, VEGAN

Nacho Mac and Cheese

Prep Time: 40 minutes | Cook Time: 15 minutes | Serves 4 | GF

I could simply not put out a cookbook without adding a macaroni and cheese recipe. Disclaimer: this is not my infamous Mac & Yease that you may have heard about. That recipe is a family secret, and my sister and I have vowed never to share it. #truestory. However, as we know, mac and cheese in America is all about your twist on it. Unlike the baked original, this version is modeled after the old blue-box brand so that you can make it quickly on the stovetop. I also chose gluten-free noodles so it's friendly for all.

Here's the hack: This recipe uses the cheese sauce and quinoa from the Loaded Quinoa Nachos (page 49) for a cheesy, hearty sauce. Throw in some corn chips for an added crunch.

Hacking order: quinoa, noodles, cheese sauce

1/2 recipe Loaded Quinoa Nachos (page 49)

1 1/2 cups gluten-free elbow macaroni

1 recipe Cheese Sauce (page 49)

1 cup crumbled corn chips, for topping

1. **Quinoa:** Follow the instructions for making the quinoa. Set aside.

2. **Noodles:** Bring 4 cups of water to a boil in a medium stock pot over high heat. Add enough salt to the water until it taste like the ocean, approximately 1 1/2 teaspoons. Add 1 tablespoon of oil to the water, then add noodles. Stir well to prevent sticking. Reduce the heat to medium-low, cover, and cook for 7 to 10 minutes or until al dente. While the macaroni is cooking, you should move on to step three. When the macaroni is done cooking, remove it from the heat and set aside, covered, for an additional 3 to 5 minutes until tender, then drain completely in a colander and return to the pot. Keep covered. The steam trapped in the pot will slowly finish cooking the macaroni

3. **Sauce and Assembly:** Follow the instructions to complete the cheese sauce. Once the cheese sauce is ready and holding at a low simmer, add the cooked noodles slowly to maintain the desired ratio of noodles to sauce. Once the noodles and sauce are well incorporated, add the quinoa and mix well. Serve hot, topped with crushed corn chips.

Moroccan Tempeh Flatbread

Prep Time: 10 minutes | Cook Time: 25 minutes | Serves 2 to 4

The way I hack recipes is to think about all the different elements that make up the dish, and break them down by function – protein, fat, flavor, carb. Then I start this slot machine type process of elimination to see how these ingredients can be remixed or switched out until ding, ding, ding! Jackpot! In this recipe hack, the tempeh is the protein, the chermoula is the main source of flavor, and the couscous is the carb. I really like the original chermoula recipe (page 132), and when brainstorming a remix I thought, I'd love to eat this dish with my hands. Why not? It's popular in that region of the world. Well, what better way to get my hands on this dish than by turning it into a twist on an American favorite: pizza? Exactly, none!

Here's the hack: This is the perfect thing to do with your leftover chermoula from last night's dinner. We're adding the tempeh and chermoula from Chapter 6 to the pizza dough from Chapter 8, along with a few fresh ingredients that you probably have laying around. Boom! New recipe.

Hacking order: pizza dough, tempeh, chermoula sauce

1/2 recipe pizza dough (omit sugar) (page 177)

1 batch Moroccan tempeh (page 132)

1 batch chermoula sauce (page 132)

1 large tomato, sliced in rounds

1/2 cup thinly sliced sweet onion

1/2 cup vegan goat cheese (optional, see Note)

1. Pizza Dough: Following instructions, prepare the pizza dough and allow it to rise for the allotted amount of time. While that is proofing, move to step two. Preheat oven to 450°F.

2. Tempeh: Following instructions, prepare the tempeh by cutting it into 1-inch x 3-inch strips (1/8-inch thick). Set aside.

3. Sauce: Follow the instructions to make the chermoula sauce. Reserve some extra chopped mint and parsley leaves for the pizza topping. Set aside.

4. Assembly: Roll out the pizza dough into a thin layer and place it on a parchment paper lined baking sheet. Bake for 15 minutes. Remove from the oven and evenly spread on the chermoula sauce across it. Layer on the tempeh, tomatoes, onions, and cheese, if using. Return the pizza to the oven and bake for 10 more minutes. Once done, remove from the oven and top with fresh mint and parsley. Cut into small squares and serve hot.

Note: One big source of my hacking is the internets. Search for a vegan goat cheese recipe—I found a couple good ones out there.

Seitan Parmesan Nuggets with Ranch Dressing

Prep Time: 10 minutes | Cook Time 20 minutes | Serves 4

Let's face it: vegans go ape sh*t over a nugget. Or at least I do. Something about them being fried, crunchy, and bite-sized. All that in a vegan package, well, it's winning. This is a great pick for kids, starters, or a quick snack for you and the bae. Couple it with the ranch dressing recipe on the next page and pow! Your kitchen is transformed into a vegan fast food spot.

Here's the hack: Take the seitan parm recipe and literally hack it to bite-sized pieces. Done and done. Well, almost...

Hacking Order: seitan, breading, ranch dressing

1 half batch Seitan Parmesan (page 142)

1 batch breading for Seitan Parmesan (page 142)

1 batch Ranch Dressing (page 209)

1 cup unsweetened soy milk

1 cup safflower oil, for frying

1. Seitan and Dredging: If you're not using leftovers from the original seitan parm recipe, then follow the instructions on page 142, and add an hour to your prep time. I suggest preparing your seitan the night before to cut about an hour off this recipe. Cut the seitan into bite size nuggets. Set up your dredging and breading bowls. Dredge the seitan nuggets in milk first, then breading. Repeat this process twice on each piece for a "double dip" dredge which provides an extra-delicious, extra-crispy outside. Once done, set aside on parchment paper. Allow the nuggets to sit for about 7 to10 minutes until the moisture soaks through the breading.

2. Ranch: Make the dressing and set aside.

3. Cooking: Line a baking sheet with paper towels and set aside. Heat the oil in a small skillet over medium-high heat until hot and shimmering. Drop the nuggets into the oil and cook until golden brown on all sides, flipping with tongs halfway through. Remove from the oil and place on the prepared baking sheet. Repeat until done. Serve hot, with the ranch dressing for dipping.

Ranch Dressing

Prep Time: 5 minutes | Serves 2 to 4

Ranch dressing is an American favorite. Here's the thing: it's a pretty basic cream base, and if you're making your own, you can add anything to make it whatever you want! This is my twist on a traditional ranch. Feel free to throw in fennel or something crazy! You're the chef now.

1 cup unsweetened soy milk

1/4 cup vegan mayonnaise

1/4 cup vegan sour cream

2 tablespoons lemon juice

3 tablespoons chopped fresh Italian parsley

3 tablespoons minced chives

1 tablespoon chopped fresh garlic

1 teaspoon smoked paprika

2 tablespoons vegan Worcestershire sauce

Salt and black pepper

In a medium bowl, whisk all ingredients thoroughly. Refrigerate until ready to serve.

HACKER IDEAS

Pour this dressing on salads, drizzle it on pizza, slather it on a sandwich, dip crudités in it, or cool down some hot vegan buffalo wings. C'mon, it's ranch! Put it on anything!

Dirty Quinoa Breakfast Burrito

Prep Time: 10 minutes | Cook Time: 10 minutes | Serves 2

The burrito or wrap is almost as well known in the veggie community as the sprout. It makes things easy: easy to make, easy to hold, and easy to eat. A breakfast burrito is arguably the best kind of burrito, since breakfast really is the most important meal.

Here's the hack: This recipe makes use of the leftover Lover's Hash, Dirty Quinoa, and Cajun Tofu. If you don't have all three chilling in the fridge already, don't sweat it.

Hacking Order: hash, quinoa, tofu

1 batch Lover's Hash (page 23)

1/2 batch Dirty Quinoa (page 134)

1 batch Cajun Tofu (page 134)

2 large tortillas

1/2 cup shredded vegan cheese

1 ripe avocado, pitted, peeled, and
   sliced (optional)

1. Hash: Follow the instructions to prepare the hash. Set aside. Keep warm.

2. Quinoa: While hash is cooking, prepare the quinoa according to the instructions. Set aside and keep warm.

3. Tofu: Follow the instructions for preparing the tofu. Set aside and keep warm.

4. Assembly: If you've ever attempted a homemade burrito and ended up with a big ol' mess on your plate, then you know this is the hard part, but fret not. The key is a warm tortilla. To heat, throw the tortillas over the hash while it's warm until the tortillas are warm to the touch. Place all the filling ingredients, one by one, ending with the cheese and avocado, onto each tortilla, leaving about 1/3 of the tortilla empty at the top. Roll the tortillas and tuck in the ends as you go to seal in all the goodness.

POOR MAN'S PANINI

Heat 1 tablespoon of oil in a medium skillet over medium heat, until hot and shimmering. Place the burritos in the skillet, seam-side down. Allow the tortilla to crisp, and flip to the other side. Cook approximately 2 minutes on either side. Ideally, this will melt the cheese and give your burrito a nice brown crispy outside. The use of a toothpick to hold the seam together is allowed.

The Best Popcorn Ever

Prep Time: 1 minutes | Cook Time 5 minutes | Serves 4 | GF, SFO

When I was working in Atlanta, I was asked by my client to pick up some artisan popcorn that was made by this lady nearby. I said okay, took the address, and dutifully went off to find this special popcorn. I end up on the, ahem, other side of town in an apartment complex that required a special knock. It was like when Neo went to see the Oracle in *The Matrix*. The lady actually looked similar. There in the apartment was a full service vegan restaurant with tables and a menu and a retail rack of this popcorn. I told her who sent me and she hurriedly got my order together. I left in amazement. The popcorn was a real treat, and though I couldn't pinpoint the exact ingredients, I knew the base was the coconut oil she popped it in, and some nutritional yeast. I improvised with the rest and it came out quite good. Enjoy. Use a soy-free vegan butter to make this soy-free.

Here's the hack: Sprinkle your hot popcorn with leftover Kale-ritos Seasoning.

Hacking order: Kale-ritos seasoning, popcorn

1 batch Kale-oritos seasoning (page 200)

2 tablespoons coconut oil

1/3 cup high-quality popcorn

1 tablespoon vegan butter (or more coconut oil)

Salt

1. Seasoning: If not using leftovers, following instructions to make the Kaleritos seasoning.

2. Popcorn: Heat the oil in a large stockpot over high heat until hot. Add the popcorn, cover and listen for the first pop. Swirl the pot over the heat as the kernels begin to pop. Keep the pot moving and when the pops start to lessen in frequency, remove from heat. The popcorn should be fluffed up near the top of the pot. Transfer the popcorn to a large bowl. Put the butter in the empty pot until it melts. Working quickly, pour the butter over the popcorn, add the Kaleritos seasoning, and salt to taste. Mix well with a spoon.

Epic Biscuits and Gravy

Prep Time: 10 minutes | Cook Time: 20 minutes | Serves 4

The thing I never liked about biscuits and gravy is that there is no protein. All carbs make Ayindé a hungry boy. So I added fried tofu to this because anyone who follows my Instagram knows I'm always posting my fried tofu in something. This seems like a no-brainer, right? Serve with some fresh fruit of your choice. I suggest something juicy, like watermelon or honeydew.

Here's the Hack: We're making use of leftover biscuits and fried tofu. Mmm, tofu.

Hacking Order: biscuits, tofu, gravy

1 batch of the biscuits (page 24)

1 batch Fried Tofu (page 161)

1 batch Mushroom Truffle Gravy (page 112)

1. Biscuits: If you don't have leftover biscuits on hand, then follow instructions to make biscuits fresh. For this hack, I like to make them bigger using my hands instead of a jar top. These are what my daddy called Hoe Cakes. I don't have the answers, just the questions.

2. Tofu: Make the tofu according to the instructions. You might want to double or triple that original recipe depending on if it's breakfast or an epic cheat day.

3. Gravy and Assembly: Following instructions, make the gravy last because hot fresh gravy is like heaven on earth. Serve biscuits on the bottom, top with tofu and cover with hot gravy in one glorious stack. You're welcome.

"Let your delicious food, high energy, and content mindset do the talking!"

– JAMEE, VEGAN

Dark Chocolate Pocky

Prep Time: 10 minutes | Cook Time: 15 minutes | Makes 12

While traveling in Korea, I had a co-worker who liked to eat everything authentic. While sitting next to me on the plane, she pulled out some pocky and offered me some. I had of course seen the chocolate-covered biscuit sticks before, but asked to see the package. After some quick Terminator-style analysis of the ingredients, I knew they weren't vegan, but thought I could recreate them with dark chocolate, because I currently do not have the technology to keep vegan milk chocolate from melting at room temp. Like those delicious Go Max Go bars. Maybe for the next book.

Here's the Hack: Wondering what to do with that leftover biscuit dough? Wonder no further!

Hacking Order: biscuits, chocolate

1/2 batch biscuit dough (page 24)

1 double batch of chocolate from the Mexican Hot Chocolate-Covered Strawberries (page 175), omitting the pepper

1. Biscuit Sticks: Preheat the oven to 425°F. Following instructions for traditional biscuits up until the shaping part. On a floured cutting board, roll out the dough into a square shape about 1/8-inch thick. Cut the dough into 1/8-inch strips, approximately 8-inches long. Use your hands to gently roll the strips until they are cylindrical. Carefully place them on a baking sheet and bake until done, about 10 minutes. Remove from the oven and allow to cool to room temperature.

2. Chocolate: Prepare two baking sheets with parchment paper and set aside. Prepare the chocolate sauce. Pour the chocolate sauce onto one of the baking sheets. Carefully roll the biscuit sticks two-thirds of the way in the chocolate so that there is still some bare biscuit sticking out at the end. Arrange them on the second prepared baking sheet. Repeat until done. Place chocolate-covered pocky in the refrigerator for at least 30 minutes to set the chocolate. Serve cold.

Meet-the-Omnis
Big-Ass Holiday Wrap

Prep Time: 10 minutes | Cook Time: 10 minutes | Serves 4

One of my favorite New York haunts, a sandwich shop called S'Nice, recently closed one of their locations. I get it, the food business is rough. But they had a particular wrap that Zoë really loved, and it just so happens that we have all the ingredients floating around this book to re-create it. So this is for all my New Yorkers who will miss the Thanksgiving wrap from the West Village location.

Here's the hack: We make use of nearly all of our holiday recipes (this is the "big ass" portion of the name), so this is the perfect thing to make the day after your holiday feast. Or at midnight that day, when all of the guests are gone, and you feel like pillaging the leftovers. No judgment.

Hacking Order: seitan, stuffing, cranberry sauce

1/2 batch Seitan Wellington (page 120)

1 tablespoon grapeseed or safflower oil

1/2 batch Quinoa Wild Rice Stuffing (page 116)

1/2 batch Vodka Cranberry Sauce (page 118)

2 large tortillas

1. Seitan: Follow the instructions to make the seitan only from the wellington recipe. If you're not using leftovers but making it just for this sammy, the seitan can be baked without the puff pastry around it. Slice approximately 8 ounces of the seitan into strips.

2. Heat the oil in a medium skillet over medium-high heat. Add the seitan and sear it on both sides, 3 to 5 minutes on each side. Set aside but keep warm.

3. Stuffing: If not using leftover stuffing, prepare the stuffing following the instructions on page 116. Set aside and keep warm.

4. Cranberry Sauce: If not using leftovers, prepare the cranberry sauce following instructions on page 118.

5. Assembly: Heat the tortillas in a skillet until warm to the touch, lay them open, and divide ingredients between the two. For best results, assemble in this order: seitan, then stuffing, then the cranberry sauce.

Mexican Spice Blend

Prep Time: 5 minutes | Serves 2 to 4 | GF, SF

When I go out to eat, I look for Mexican. Why? Because, vegan or not, it's hard to mess up Mexican. The flavors are so rich and robust, you could put cumin and chili on an old shoe, and it would taste good. What I mean is, I know any cook—both the great and the half-assed—can impress with the knowledge of how to use cumin and bit of chili pepper. Don't forget to serve your final product with a lime wedge. Anything slightly Mexican-flavored tastes exponentially better with lime. Corona, anyone?

1 1/2 tablespoons chile powder

2 tablespoons ground cumin

1 tablespoon rubbed sage

1 teaspoon smoked paprika

In a small bowl, combine the chile powder, cumin, sage, and paprika. Mix well.

Eating ideas: You can use this to jazz up a can of plain refried beans, or add it to some fried rice or cooked quinoa. Sprinkle it on top of a salad for a fiesta feel, or blend it into some vegan mayo to make an awesome dip for a party tray of chips or veggies. Homemade dip? Yeah, you got that.

Trinidadian Pepper Sauce

Prep time: 5 minutes | Serves: 2 to 4 | GF, SF

I'm a bit of a hot sauce connoisseur. As any connoisseur knows, it's all about the flavor, and with hot sauce it's often the balance of acid and sweet and the flavor of the individual chile pepper that make it amazing. I was traveling in Trinidad and Tobago with India.Arie, and while looking for new ingredients as I always do in new environments, I kept seeing these beautiful chiles. Intrigued, I tasted some of the local hot sauce and was blown away. I wanted to make my own version, and was insistent on using very few ingredients to keep it similar to the real deal. Here is what I came up with.

2 Trinidadian hot chile peppers or Scotch bonnet chiles

Juice of 2 limes

1 tablespoon agave nectar

1/4 teaspoon salt

1. Using plastic gloves, mince the chiles, reserving the seeds. Transfer to a bowl. Add more seeds for more heat, if desired.

2. Add the lime juice, agave, and salt. Mix well and serve.

Eating Ideas: If you're into hot sauce, you know the answer: Put that sh*t on everything.

We Hate Good-Byes

ZOË: My experiences in love and sex have taught me that finding a true connection is more important to me than finding a true vegan. I can be vegan enough for the both of us. That being said, my last little advice nugget is basic:

Watch how you talk to your partner about veganism.

Actually, watch how you talk to everybody about veganism. This is a universal suggestion. I can be the queen of Always Right, and this doesn't usually lead to positive conversations when the person I'm talking to downright disagrees with me. Especially when they're just bloody wrong,

and clearly I am right, and...dammit, there I go again. Seriously, I have spent years trying to work on this. It's an ongoing battle for me but here are two tricks that seem to produce the best results. These techniques are simple but not necessarily easy, and they work for all important conversations, not just food politics.

Instead of telling them your opinion, ask thoughtful questions about their opinions. Ask them to think differently, and when similarly challenged, be ready to think differently yourself. Sometimes, in order to understand someone else's opinion, you need to think outside of your own. Far, far outside. In Jonathan Safran Foer's Eating Animals (the book that turned Daniel vegetarian!), Foer facetiously makes the argument that if we absolutely have to eat animals to survive in modern America, then we should be eating dogs, as we already euthanize thousands of them every day. Now, mind you, Foer doesn't really think we should eat dogs, he was just making a point about American's relationships with animals, and asking us to think differently, The initial shock (and outrage) most of us experience at the thought of eating Fido is something worth ruminating on for anyone who has previously scoffed at veganism. I'm not saying you need to tell your omni partner to eat dogs—simply ask them to stretch outside of their mental comfort zone.

Listen. Listening is a skill that needs to be curated, and it's much different than simply biting your tongue and waiting for your turn to speak. Absorb your partner's thoughts and feelings. Digest them. Think about them. And then rebut.

AYINDE: Here are my last two cents on the matter.

On love. I really want to tell you everything—all I have learned—in hopes that it helps you in some way. But like in relationships, some things slip through the cracks. I know I forgot something that will change your life! So in an attempt to avoid that, I am going to give you the most basic advice about love: you know it when you feel it—if it's not a yes, it's a no.

On veganism and cooking. When you become vegan and want to eat good food, the first thing to do is have the proper ingredients in your kitchen. Sometimes you may have to shop at different supermarkets or, at the very least, different aisles in your current supermarket. Most major supermarket chains have the ingredients you need to make all the dishes in this book. If you can't find them, another resource is Amazon or any other online vegan specialty foods retailer.

As a restaurant-trained chef, I have learned to integrate my seasonings and sauces into different meals to save time and space and help use up leftovers. The recipes in this book use great basic sauce and seasoning recipes that also work well as dips, dressings, and marinades, and for creating your own fantastic meals. Be creative and hack on. With all these goodies in your pantry and this advice in your head, you can't go wrong! Until next time, be well, cook good, and make more vegan babies! Say bye, Zoë.

ZOË: Well, I hope that was as good for you as it was for me. While you're freshening up in the bathroom, I will blindly grope the floor for my undies and make a mad dash for the door...just kidding. We can snuggle.

Real talk: I hope you were able to learn something from this book, whether it's a new favorite recipe or a new way to approach your relationships—current, past, or future. Because if you're not learning, you're not growing, and what's life without growth? Boring as all f*ck, that's what.

If you take only one morsel of truth away from this book, I hope it is this: You can't get into a relationship expecting someone to change. While it would be terrific if they took to tofu for you and for their own health and the world, expectations like that will only lead to disappointment and resentment. As the vegan or the omnivore, all you can hope is that your partner will accept you, and maybe make a few tweaks to ensure everyone is comfortable. And if you expect them to tweak, then you have to be willing to do it as well.

With that in mind, I would like to close with a saying I see on bumper stickers everywhere and wish I had written myself:

Love people, and cook them tasty (vegan) food.

Acknowledgments

We would like to thank our iEatGrass.com team for all of their efforts and hard work on the site as we put this book together: Shadé Ibe, Elyssa Schwartz and Lindsay Geller, as well as all of our interns, past, present and future. We would also like to thank *The Lusty Vegan*'s culinary intern, Chef Kaila West; our wonderful photographer Geoff Souder for cramming into every spot imaginable for the right shot; our incredible models, Naomi Henderson and Phillips Payson; all of our fantastic recipe testers; our agent JL Stermer and the rest of the team at N.S. Bienstock; our publisher Jon Robertson for seeing our vision and taking us on; all of Ayinde's clients and customers that supported him from Hillside Quickies Vegan Sandwich Shop in Seattle, to Jivamuktea Cafe in NYC, as well as all his pop-up restaurant patrons at Wildflower, Petit Déjeuner, and The Lusty Vegan; and all of our iEatGrass.com readers—we couldn't have done it without you. No, really.

About the Authors

Ayindé Howell has over fifteen years' experience as a restaurant chef, beginning when he opened his first café in Seattle in 1999. After five years and notable success in Seattle, he took his show on the road to New York, becoming an executive chef, one of the youngest in Manhattan. Ayindé has since traveled the world cooking vegan vittles for celebrities. His recipes have been published in the *New York Times*, *Essence Magazine*, *VegNews Magazine*, and many others. He is a fourth generation entrepreneur who currently holds the position of founder and "Bossman" of the award-winning website iEatGrass.com, also home to his critically acclaimed culinary event brand, Wildflower. He currently lives and works in Hollywood, California, cooking meals and planning for vegan multi-media world domination.

Websites: Ieatgrass.com, thelustyvegan.com, and ayindehowell.com
Twitter: @ayinde @ieatgrassdotcom
Instagram: @ayinde @ieatgrassdotcom
Pinterest: ieatgrassdotcom
Facebook: facebook.com/ayindehowell and facebook.com/ieatgrass

With a background in creative writing and health promotion, **Zoë Eisenberg** has spent the last five years working in the publishing industry as both a writer and an editor. A certified holistic health counselor, Zoë enjoys writing about health, wellness, relationships and sexuality. Her work has appeared in a variety of online and print publications, including the Huffington Post, xoJane.com, Shape.com, Thought Catalog, and *Laika Magazine*. Zoë posts regularly about living, loving, and eating on her blog, SexyTofu.com, and is presently the managing editor of iEatGrass.com. In her free time, Zoë moonlights as a screenwriter, and has written and produced several independent feature and short films. Zoë currently lives, works, and plays on the big island of Hawaii. This is her first book.

Websites: www.zoeeisenberg.com, www.sexytofu.com, www.thelustyvegan.com
Twitter: www.twitter.com/sexytofublog
Instagram: www.instagram.com/zoahu

About the Photographer

Geoff Souder is Los Angeles-based photographer and the founder of ZE Photography. A vegan, Geoff likes to spread compassion through visual storytelling. He specializes in food photography, yoga, and both animal and human portraiture. See his work at www.ze-photo.com.

Index